بسم الله الرحمن الرحيم

الحمد لله رب العالمين

والصلاة والسلام على خاتم الأنبياء والمرسلين

In the Name of Allah,
the Compassionate, the Merciful,
Praise be to Allah, Lord of the Universe,
and Peace and Prayers be upon
His Final Prophet and Messenger.

بِسْمِ ٱللَّهِ ٱلرَّحْمَٰنِ ٱلرَّحِيمِ

ٱقْرَأْ بِٱسْمِ رَبِّكَ ٱلَّذِى خَلَقَ ﴿١﴾ خَلَقَ ٱلْإِنسَٰنَ مِنْ عَلَقٍ ﴿٢﴾
ٱقْرَأْ وَرَبُّكَ ٱلْأَكْرَمُ ﴿٣﴾ ٱلَّذِى عَلَّمَ بِٱلْقَلَمِ ﴿٤﴾ عَلَّمَ ٱلْإِنسَٰنَ
مَا لَمْ يَعْلَمْ ﴿٥﴾

(العلق: ١ ـ ٥)

Read in the name of your Sustainer, Who has Created man out of a germ cell. Read – for your Sustainer is the Most bountiful One. Who has taught (man) the use of the pen. Taught Man what he did not know.

(Qur'an 96:1-5)

وَٱللَّهُ أَخْرَجَكُم مِّنۢ بُطُونِ أُمَّهَٰتِكُمْ لَا تَعْلَمُونَ شَيْـًٔا
وَجَعَلَ لَكُمُ ٱلسَّمْعَ وَٱلْأَبْصَٰرَ وَٱلْأَفْـِٔدَةَ
لَعَلَّكُمْ تَشْكُرُونَ ﴿٧٨﴾

(النحل: ٧٨)

And Allah has brought you forth from your mother's womb knowing nothing – but He has endowed you with hearing, and sight, and minds, so that you might have cause to be grateful.

(Qur'an 16:78)

ISLAMIC AWAKENING
BETWEEN
REJECTION *AND* EXTREMISIM

First Edition
(1407–1987)

Second Revised Edition
(1412–1991)

ISLAMIC AWAKENING
BETWEEN
REJECTION *AND* EXTREMISM

Yūsuf al Qaraḍāwi,

New English Edition Revised and Edited by

A. S. Al Shaikh-Ali, Ph.D.
Mohamed B. E. Wasfy

Jointly Published by

American Trust Publication
and
The International Institute of Islamic Thought

ISSUES IN ISLAMIC THOUGHT (2)

Library of Congress Cataloging-in-Publication Data

Al Qaraḍāwī, Yūsuf. 1926 (1344) -
[Al Ṣaḥwah al Islāmīyah bayna al Juḥūd wa al Taṭarruf]. Islamic Awakening between Rejection & Extremism/Yūsuf al Qaraḍāwī. – New English ed./revised and edited by A. S. Al Shaikh-Ali, Mohamed B. E. Wasfy.

p. cm.—(Issues of Islamic thought series; no. 2)

Translation of: *Al Ṣaḥwah al Islāmīyah bayna al Juḥūd wa al Taṭarruf.* Includes bibliographical references

ISBN 0-912463-52-X

1. Islam—20th century. I. Al Shaikh-Ali, A.S. II. Wasfy, Mohamed B. E. III. Title. IV. Title: Islamic awakening between rejection and extremism. V.-Series.

BP163.Q2713 1990 90-4996
297'.09'04—dc20 CIP

Printed in the United States of America
by International Graphics Printing Services
4411 41st Street
Brentwood, Maryland 20722 U.S.A.
Tel. (301) 779-7774 Fax (301) 779-0570

Contents

Chapter One

Chapter Two

Chapter Three

Chapter Four

Indices

Preface to the Second Edition

Tackling the subject of extremism is a very difficult enterprise. To attempt to do so in the case of Islam in the eighties is an almost hazardous task—at least one fraught with likely traps. Dr. Yūsuf al Qaraḍāwī is well aware of this issue for he admits in his introduction to this book that he hesitated to open a dialogue on religious extremism "for fear that what I may write, especially these days, could be misinterpreted or even deliberately explained to serve something contrary to my intentions...".

Unfortunately, his caution is well founded, for there are groups ready to use any such internal Islamic debate to protect or further their vested interest in the present postnationalism period. While reaction agains such groups has helped to radicalize extremism in the last decade or so, the main reasons of extremism lie elsewhere.

In its essence, extremism is the direct outcome of a deficiency in thinking. Religious extremism is the antithesis of *da'wah* and therefore should not exist in normal conditions. Although it is in part a reaction against oppression, it has also resulted from a deficient or distorted knowledge of the basic sources of Islam, a subject Dr. al Qaraḍāwī has discussed with great skill and insight. For historical reasons not convenient to outline here, the cessation of *ijtihād* resulted in the rise and eventual domination of *taqlīd* (blind following and imitation), a very damaging and negative development which still afflicts vast areas of the Ummah in our own day. The Muslims' adherence to *taqlīd* has led to a distortion of Islam's mission, to a stagnation of thought and, as a result of this, to approaches to the Qur'an and the Sunnah which do not take into account changes coming about due to the passage of time and evolving social conditions. It is in such a situation that the eternal validity of the Qur'an for all peoples is blocked: opinions, interpretations, and decisions made on a particular issue, in a particular circumstance, at a particular time are strongly adhered to and considered the solution *par excellence* for similar issues in our time. Such an intellectual discrepancy brings about a shunning of *ijtihād,* a concentration on minor issues at the expense of major ones, and breeds divisions and strife. Focusing on non-issues deprives Islam of its claim of being a viable and global alternative way of life, thus depreciating its real dimension in the eyes of humanity and engendering increased hostility towards Islam and Muslims worldwide.

It was this intellectual deficiency and these mistaken attitudes which Dr. al Qaraḍāwī's book sought to address when it was first published in the early 1980s. In fact, as far back as the 1970s, many Muslim thinkers who were aware of the need to reform Islamic thought engaged in a program of concerted action which resulted in the establishment of the International Institute of Islamic Thought in 1401/1981.

Convinced that the Ummah's problems are mere products of the prevailing malaise and that intellectual deviation and stagnation have impaired Muslim thought, the Institute has striven relentlessly to mobilize enlightened thinkers and to encourage research and production in the field of Islamic thought. This endeavor has already borne some remarkable fruits. After the present book, Dr. al Qaraḍāwī wrote *Kayfa Nata'āmal ma'a al Sunnah al Nabawīyah* **(Methods of Understanding the Sunnah),** while Shaikh Muhammad al Ghazālī published *Kayfa Nata'āmal ma'a al Qur'ān,* **(Methods of Understanding the Qur'an).** For their part, Dr. Ṭāhā Jābir al 'Alwānī, Dr. 'AbdulḤamīd AbūSulaymān, Dr. 'Imād al Dīn Khalīl, Dr. Muḥammad 'Umārah as well as many other scholars have produced books and have regularly contributed many papers on Islamic thought to the Institute's co-publications: the *American Journal of Islamic Social Sciences* (AJISS) and *Al Muslim al Mu'āṣir.* In the *Occasional Papers* series of the Institute, *The Qur'an and the Sunnah: The Time-Space Factor* by Dr. Tāhā Jābir al 'Alwānī and Dr. 'Imad al Dīn Khalīl has recently been published. Dr. al 'Alwānī's articles on *ijtihād* serialized in AJISS as well as the forthcoming *Occasional Paper* on the subject are orginal and timely contributions.

The second English edition of the present book appears in the wake of the second devastating Gulf war for the Muslim world, a war whose far-reaching consequences threathen the Ummah's very fabric. This war has laid bare the shortenings and shortsightedness of Islamic movements worldwide: their deviations, contradictions, and cracks were translated into hasty, immature, desperate, and even calculated stands and emotional attitudes. In a word, they proved to suffer from a clear want of intellectual and political awareness. Such shortcomings, which are the result of the Islamic movements' failure to reconsider their eductional and intellectual programs, were foretold in Dr. al Qaraḍāwī's book when it was first published in the early 1980s.

Although the first English edition of *Islamic Awakening* suffered from serious editorial problems, it proved very popular especially among the Muslim youth. As demands increased, the Institute decided to produce a new edition. *In shā'a Allah*, the new release of this book will once again be of great benefit to young Muslims, especially those who are disappointed with many of the established Islamic movements' and parties' inadequate response to the prevailing challenges. They have also become restless about their internecine disputes and dissatisfied with many scholars' inability to keep pace with social change in terms of awarness of the time-space factor. Finally the youth, if rightly guided, will have a good chance to grasp the unaviodable need to adapt to the modern world while firmly holding onto and nurturing their civilizational and spiritual specificity. It is therefore hoped that the older generation and leaders will also benefit from the book by becoming clearly aware of their shortcomings and the critical stage through which the Ummah is currently passing. An enlightened guidance of the youth as well as the Islamic movements is urgently needed.

The warnings and recommendations of Dr. al Qaraḍāwī, which may have beem overlooked before, are bound to be heeded and appreciated in light of the current ominous situation and in view of the difficult but necessary adjustments Islamic movements must undergo if they are to effectively serve their Ummah and solve its problems.

International Institute of Islamic Thought
Herndon, Virginia

Jumādā al Ākhirah 1412 AH
December 1991 AC

Preface to the First Edition

The International Institute of Islamic Thought and American Trust Publications are pleased to present this book to our readers in the English language. We have chosen it because of our concern for the future of the Ummah, Islamic thought, and Muslim youth.

The author, Dr. Yūsuf al Qaraḍāwī, is famous for *al Ḥalāl wa al Ḥarām fī al Islām,* published in English by American Trust Publications under the title *The Lawful and the Prohibited in Islām.* Dr. al Qaraḍāwī has extensive experience in the field of *da'wah* and is recognized as an authority in Islamic *'aqīdah* (belief) and Sharī'ah.

Allah (SWT) has entrusted this Ummah with a great mission to lead humanity to the right path of truth, justice, and progress. It is unfortunate that Muslims have been struggling but have not been able to fulfil this mission for the last few centuries. Allah (SWT) has been generous in bestowing upon Muslims tremendous human and material resources, but they have not been able to mobilize them effectively enough to influence the flow of current events in the direction of peace and prosperity for mankind.

The extraordinary pressures, internal decadence, and challenges of the modern age have tried the patience of Muslim youth. The great Islamic vision has become blurred, and the socioeconomic and political life of the Ummah has become fragmented and stagnanted. Muslim youth have pride and confidence in Islam, but with their limited experience and knowledge they tend to take desperate and extreme courses of action. They are swayed by misdirected, short-sighted, and superficial slogans. The suffering of the youth has inflicted more suffering and pain on the Ummah, wasted their valuable energy, and undermined Islamic leadership still further.

This is an outstanding work by an outstanding scholar, *dā'īyah,* and educator. It helps the youth to reconstruct the total picture of the history and the destiny of the Ummah. It deals with the Qur'ān and *Sunnah* in a balanced and comprehensive manner and provides a very constructive approach for Muslim youth to study the Qur'ān and *Sunnah* and benefit from them.

This book helps to analyze systematically and objectively the causes of the crises faced by Muslim youth and presents the ways and means Muslims should adopt to seek solutions. The different aspects of the Ummah and the proper Islamic way to resolve its crises are clarified. From this book the reader can gain a wealth of experience and Islamic knowledge.

Furthermore, the book is a great help to Muslim youth in developing right approaches to the challenges and pressures of the modern age in order to achieve the Islamic goals and objectives. This is recommended reading for every Muslim youth, intellectual, and scholar.

International Institute of Islamic Thought
American Trust Publications
Herndon Virginia
1407 AH/1987 AC

Introduction

In Ramaḍān and Shawwāl 1401 AH/1981 AC, *al Ummah* magazine published my two-part article on the awakening of Muslim youth.[1] In this study I drew attention to the positive and negative aspects which concerned observers, *du'āh*[2] and Muslim scholars attributed to the awakening. I also suggested that we should have a dialogue with and show paternal sympathy toward these young Muslims, and then channel their reawakening in order to strengthen rather than to impoverish Islam. The response to this study was so warm throughout the Muslim world that the study was translated into several languages. Furthermore, the youth in many Muslim universities tolerantly studied my views despite the fact that my views were critical of many of them.

I would like here to acknowledge with pleasure the attitude of the Islamic Group at the University of Cairo who adopted my study during their ninth camp in the summer of 1981 and printed and distributed it to all those interested. This indeed reflects a laudable awareness as well as a readiness to support moderation.

I shall not indulge here in discussing the recent events which occurred in some Muslim countries and which involved serious and bloody confrontation between the youth and the authorities, not only because I do not want to aggravate the matter further, but also because *al Ummah* magazine has always catered to the whole Muslim Ummah,[3] not any particular group. What concerns us here is the prolonged and heated discussion aroused by these events on so-called "religious extremism," in which not only learned people participated but also those whose knowledge of Islam is characterized by ignorance and whose attitude is characterized by animosity, sarcasm, and cynicism.

---

1 Al Qaraḍāwī, "The Awakening of Muslim Youth Is a Salutary Phenomenon to be Guided Not Resisted," *al Ummah* Magazine (1981).

2 *Dā'iyah* (pl. *du'ah):* "Caller to Islam."

3 Ummah: "The community as identified by its ideology, law, religion, its group consciousness, ethics and mores, culture and art."

I was also asked a few years ago by *al 'Arabī* magazine to write on the subject of "religious extremism" with special emphasis on its true nature and its characteristics. When the article appeared in the special edition of January 1982, some friends blamed me for contributing to an issue where the truth, they believed, was being generally distorted in support of *bāṭil.*[4] Although my friends did not question either the contents or the essence of the article, they were nevertheless suspicious of the motives and aims behind the campaign which has lately been launched against "religious extremisim." They were not convinced that the campaign genuinely sought to resist extremism or to guide the extremists to the path of moderation, but rather that is sought to crush the Islamic reawakening before it could become strong and popular enough to ultimately assume a significant political role. My friends noted that the authorities did not begin to pay attention to the religious youth until the latter began to oppose, on religious grounds, some of the government's policies. This is supported by the fact that the people in power actually patronized certain religious groups which had demonstrated extreme trends in order to use them against other Islamic movements, then crushed the former when their appointed role was over. As such, my friends insisted, the reasons behind the confrontation between the authorities and the Islamic groups could not be the emergence of extremism. They further believed that the authorities in our Muslim countries considered the Islamic movement a most dangerous enemy. Such authorities could, and did make alliances with either the extreme right or left, but never with the Islamic movement. Sometimes a temporary truce was declared with this movement; at other times the authorities tried to involve it in confrontation with their own political and ideological opponents. Eventually the authorities and the opponents discovered that they had more affinity of aims and means than they realized, and therefore united against the Islamic movement. Allah (SWT) says in the Qur'ān[5]: "Verily, the wrongdoers are protectors to one another, but Allah is the protector of the pious who fear Him and avoid evil" (45:19).[6] Recent events support

---

4 *Bāṭil:* "Falsehood."

5 Al Qur'ān al Karīm (the Qur'ān): The final revelation of Allah's will to the Prophet Muḥammad (ṢA'AS), conveyed in Arabic and relayed to his companions, memorized verbatim and publicly and continuously recited by them and their descendants to the present time.

6 Unless otherwise indicated, all quotations are from A. Yūsuf 'Alī's translation of the meaning of the Qur'ān.

this very strongly. The emergences of Islamic groups in Egypt was characterized by extremism. However, they eventually began to show a temperate and moderate attitude thanks to the efforts of a variety of Muslim thinkers and *du'āh* who managed to influence the thinking as well as the conduct of these young Muslims to the extent that temperance and moderation became characteristic traits of the majority of them. Surprisingly, the people in power kept silent when extremism was dominant, but crushed these groups when moderation prevailed.

I was not unware of these disheartening considerations. In fact, they made me begin my article in *al 'Arabī*[7] with the following:

> Despite my conviction of the noble aim which motivated *al 'Arabī* to open a dialogue on what has come to be known as "religious extremism," and despite my unshakable belief in the importance of the issue and the gravity of its impact on our contemporary affairs, I will not conceal the fact that I hesitated at the beginning for fear that what I may write, especially these days, could be misinterpreted or even deliberately exploited to serve something contrary to my intentions or to that of the journal itself.
>
> Moreover, "religious extremism" is currently in the dock and a target of accusations and criticism by writers and by orators. I do not like to side with the strong against the weak, and it is a fact that the authority is always in a stronger position than its opponents. Suffice it to say that an Islamist does not even enjoy the right to defend himself. There is no freedom of expression in the media, nor can he even use the platform of the mosque for that purpose.
>
> My hesitation was strengthened by the fact that for decades Islamists have been flooded with accusations by their opponents. They are labelled "reactionaries," "die-hard traditionalists," "bigots," "agents" of enemy countries, although no observer can fail to see that both the East and the West and the right and the left are united in their hostility to them and look for any opportunity to crush the Islamic awakening.
>
> However, after much thought I concluded that the issue con-

[7] The editor omitted significant paragraphs, but did not change the core of my argument.

> cerns the whole Muslim world and not a single country; that silence is not a solution, and that refusal to contribute is, like fleeing a battle, un-Islamic. I have therefore put my trust in Allah (SWT) and decided to clarify the truth. The Prophet (ṢA'AS)[8] said in a hadith:[9] "The reward of deeds depends upon intentions, and every person will get the reward according to what he has intended."[10]

Many writers who are either ignorant driven by ulterior motives, or who have no insight into the nature of the issue have felt free to voice their opinions. Such a situation inevitably invites all Muslim scholars to throw their weight behind the campaign and confront the issue in order to clarify the truth.

My determination was further strengthened by my long interest in the issue of "religious extremism." A few years ago I published an article in *al Muslim al Mu'āṣir* on "The Phenomenon of Excessive *Takfīr*."[11] Another article, "The Reawakening of Muslim Youth", mentioned earlier, was published several months ago in *al Ummah*. In addition, I have had the opportunity to meet many young Muslims face to face in their camps and during their seminars, and also to discuss with them issues that focus on one theme—the call for moderation and the warning against extremism. However, what I wrote in *al 'Arabī* was limited to the specific topic required by the journal as well as the limited space allocated for it.

For these reasons, I have for some time felt obliged to return to this issue, the phenomenon of "religious extremism", and to conduct an objective study of its reality, causes, and remedy within a genuine Islamic framework. My determination to go ahead will not be discouraged by the participation of those who seek to distort and exploit the issue. The Prophet (ṢA'AS) said: "[The banner of Islamic] knowledge will be carried from one generation to the other by the moderates who defend it against the distortion of bigots, the claims of falsafiers, and the misinter-

---

[8] *Ṣalla Allāhu 'Alayhi wa Sallam:* "May the peace and blessing of Allah be upon him." Said whenever the name of the Prophet Muḥammad (ṢA'AS) is mentioned, or whenever he is referred to as the Prophet of Allah.

[9] Hadith (pl. *Aḥādīth):* "The verbalized form of a tradition of the Prophet Muḥammad (ṢA'AS) constitutive of his *Sunnah.*"

[10] Reported by al Bukhārī and Muslim.

[11] *Kāfir* (pl. *kuffār/kafirūn):* "The person guilty of declaring solemnly his/her disbelief: *Kufr:* "The act of declaring solemnly disbelief." *Takfīr:* "To declare that a person is *kāfir.*"

pretation of the ignorant." This hadith pinpoints the duty of the learned who should clarify, not conceal, the truth so that they may avoid Allah's curse. But the responsibilty extends to various other parties who are concerned directly or indirectly with the issue under discussion.

It is neither just nor honest to hold only the young responsible for being excessive in thought or in conduct. Many others, especially those who have neglected their commitment to Islam and its teachings, share this responsibility, although they always try to exonerate themselves. Nominal Muslims, whether parents, teachers, scholars or others, have made Islam, Islamists, and *du'āh* outcasts in Muslim lands. It is strange that we readily disapprove of extremism among the young but fail to recognize our own extremism, our negligence, and our laxity. We ask the young to show temperance and wisdom, to relinquish extremism and excessiveness, but we never ask the elderly to purify themselves from hypocrisy, lying, cheating, and all forms of self-contradiction. We demand everything of our youth, but we do not practice what we preach, as if we are naturally entitled to all the rights while the young must be burdened with all the duties. Yet we always emphasize that there are duties as well as rights for all. What we actually need is the unflinching courage to admit that our youth have been forced to resort to what we call "religious extremism" through our own misdeeds. We claim to be Muslims yet we do not follow the teachings of Islam. We recite the Qur'ān but we do not apply its *aḥkām.*[12] We claim to love the Prophet Muḥammad (ṢA'AS) but we fail to follow his Sunnah.[13] We declare in our constitutions that Islam is the offical religion but we never give Islam its due place in government legislation or orientation. Our own hypocrisy and self-contradictions have alienated the young, who have sought to understand Islam without assistance or guidance from us. They have found parents discouraging, *'ulamā'*[14] indifferent, rulers hostile, and counselors cynical. Therefore, in order to rectify this situation, we need to begin by reforming ourselves and our societies according to Allah's decree before we can ask our youth to be calm, to show wisdom and temperance.

It may be worthwhile here to draw attention to a point on which those in authority, as well as some writers, usually concentrate: the duty and

---

[12] *Aḥkām:* "Prescriptions directly taken from Qur'ānic texts."

[13] Sunnah: "The Path and example of the Prophet Muḥammad (ṢA'AS), consisting of all that he said, did, approved of, or condemned.

[14] *'Ālim* (pl. *'Ulamā'):* an "Islamic scholar."

the role of the "official" religious establishments in eradicating extremism and in guiding the Islamic reawakening among our youth. Some hold these "official" religious establishments reponsible for what has happened—and is still happening—as well as for all forms of extremism and deviation. It appears that despite their importance and deep roots, these establishments are now incapable of carrying out the mission entrusted to them unless the political authorities cease to manipulate and exploit them, using them as instruments of support and praise for official policies. The official religious establishments in the Muslim world could indeed play a positive role by giving guidance and genuine Islamic knowledge to the youth if they were free to manage their own affairs without interference from people in power. However, in the absence of that freedom they remain lifeless skeletons.

We must also remember that advice is meaningless unless the adviser enjoys the trust of the youth. In the absence of such essential mutual trust and confidence, every advice given is reduced to mere rhetoric. Our young people have no faith in these religious establishments or in their leaders who have been appointed by the authorities. There were circumstances and reasons which actually convinced the youth that these establishments do not reflect the teachings of Sharī'ah,[15] but have merely become the mouthpiece of the regime. Such establishments can, therefore, exert influence only when they put their own houses in order. They should refuse to enter the ever-changing, vicious circle of politics; rather their activities should center on the upbringing of generations of *fuqahā'*[16] well-versed in Islam, and fully conscious of, and having insight into, the problems of their age, i.e., "those who convey the message of Allah, and fear none save Him" (33:39).

Our modern contemporary societies urgently need such righteous scholars who are blessed with insight and who can instruct our young people in their faith and give proper guidance to the Islamic awakening. Those who stand aloof and who are indifferent to the Islamic resurgence or who criticize it without sharing its sufferings or feeling its aspirations as well as its disappointments cannot play a positive role in its guidance. One of our ancient poets wrote:

> "None knows well the sting of craving, nor the pains of longing except he who suffers to no avail."

---

[15] Sharī'ah: "The collective name of all the laws of Islam, including Islam's whole religious, liturgical, ethical, and jurisprudential systems."

[16] *Faqīh* (pl. *Fuqahā'*): Synonymous with *'ālim*.

Those who do not live for Islam and for its spreading and do not share the suffering and the hardships that beset the Ummah are self-centered. Such people have no right to tell those who believe in Islam and live by it that they are wrong and should change; and if they seize that right by force, no one will ever listen to them.

In conclusion, my own advice to whoever undertakes to counsel the youth is to abandon his ivory towers, forsake his intellectual heritage, and come down to earth with the young. He should identify with their great expectations, warmth of affection, genuine determination, noble motivation, and good deeds. Furthermore, he must also distinguish between their negative and positive conduct and attitudes so that he can give advice based on insight, and make judgements based on evidence.

May Allah (SWT) guard us all against excessiveness and extremism and direct us toward the straight path.

Yūsuf al Qaraḍāwī
Shawwal 1402 AH
August 1982 AC

CHAPTER ONE

Extremism:
The Accusation and the Truth

Logicians argue that one cannot pass a judgment on something unless one has a clear conception of it, because the unknown and the undefined cannot be judged. Therefore, we first have to determine what "religious extremism" means before we can condemn or applaud it. We can do so by considering its reality and its most distinguishing characteristics. Literally, extremism means being situated at the farthest possible point from the center. Figuratively, it indicates a similar remoteness in religion and thought, as well as behavior. One of the main consequences of extremism is exposure to danger and insecurity.[1] Islam, therefore, recommends moderation and balance in everything: in belief, *'ibādah,*[2] conduct, and legislation. This is the straightforward path that Allah (SWT) calls *al ṣirāṭ al mustaqīm,*[3] one distinct from all the others which are followed by those who earn Allah's anger and those who go astray. Moderation, or balance, is not only a general characteristic of Islam, it is a fundamental landmark. The Qur'ān says:

> Thus have we made of you an Ummah justly balanced, that you might be witnesses over the nations, and the Messenger a witness over yourselves...(2:143).

As such, the Muslim Ummah is a nation of justice and moderation; it witnesses every deviation from the 'straightforward path' in this life and in the hereafter. Islamic texts call upon Muslims to excerise moderation and to reject and oppose all kinds of extremism: *ghulūw* (excessiveness), *tanaṭṭu'* (trangressing; meticulous religiosity) and *tashdīd* (strictness;

---

[1] This notion was expressed in a couplet (quoted in the Arabic text) by an Arabian poet who believed that his tribe was safe and a haven before becoming vulnerable when nibbled by calamities and forces into an extreme position.

[2] The act or action of serving Allah (SWT).

[3] *Al ṣirāṭ al mustaqīm:* "The straight path," *al ṣirāṭ:* "The straight path of righteousness which Allah (SWT) has revealed to the Prophet (ṢAAS) for the guidance of humanity, usually joined to the epithet *al mustaqīm.*"

austerity). A close examination of such texts shows that Islam emphatically warns against, and discourages, *ghulūw.* Let us consider the following *aḥādīth:*

1. "Beware of excessiveness in religion. [People] before you have perished as a result of [such] excessiveness."[4] The people referred to above are the people of other religions, especially *Ahl al Kitāb* [the People of the Book]; Jews and Christians and mainly the Christians. The Qur'ān addresses these people:

> Say: "O People of the Book! Exceed not in your religion the bounds [of what is proper], trespassing beyond the truth, nor follow the vain desires of people who went wrong in times gone by who misled many, and strayed [themselves] from the even Way" (5:77).

Muslims have therefore been warned not to follow in their steps: he who learns from the mistakes of others indeed lives a happier life. Furthermore, the reason behind the above ḥadīth is to alert us to the fact that *ghulūw* may crop up as an insignificant action which we then unwittingly allow to continue and develop into a menace. After reaching Muzdalifah—during his last *ḥajj*[5]—the Prophet (ṢAAS) requested Ibn 'Abbās to gather some stones for him. Ibn 'Abbās selected small stones. Upon seeing the stones, the Prophet (ṢAAS) approved of their size and said: "Yes, with such [stones do stone Satan]. Beware of excessiveness in religion."[6] This clearly indicates that Muslims should not be so zealous as to believe that using larger stones is better, thus gradually allowing excessiveness to creep into their lives. Al Imām Ibn Taymīyah argues that this warning against excessiveness applies to all forms of belief, worship, and transaction, and notes that since the Christians are more excessive in faith and in practice than any other sect, Allah (SWT) admonishes them in the Qur'ān. "Do not exceed the limits of your religion" (4:171).

2. "Ruined were those who indulged in *tanaṭṭu*." And he [the Prophet (ṢAAS)] repeated this thrice.[7] Imām al Nawawī said that the people refer-

---

[4] Reported by Aḥmad, al Nasā'ī, and Ibn Mājah in their *Sunan.*

[5] *Ḥajj:* The fifth pillar of Islam, consisting of *nīyah, iḥram, tawāf, wuqūf, uḍḥīyah,* and *rajm*—acts performed at Makkah on the ninth and tenth days of *Dhū al Ḥijjah,* the last month of the lunar year in the Islamic calendar.

[6] Reported by al Imām Aḥmad, in his *Musnad,* al Nasā'ī and Ibn Kathīr in their *Sunan,* and al Ḥākim in his *Mustadrak,* on the authority of Ibn 'Abbās.

[7] Reported by Muslim. Al Suyūṭī attributed this ḥadīth to both Aḥmad and Abū Dāwūd.

red to here, "those indulging in *tanaṭṭu*," i.e., those who go beyond the limit in their utterance as well as in their action. Evidently the above two *aḥādīth* emphatically assert that the consequence of excessiveness and zealotry will be the complete loss of this life and of the hereafter.

3. The Prophet (ṢAAS) used to say: "Do not overburden yourselves, lest you perish. People [before you] overburdened themselves and perished. Their remains are found in hermitages and monasteries."[8] Indeed, Prophet Muḥammad (ṢAAS) always condemned any tendency toward religious excessiveness. He cautioned those of his companions who were excessive in *'ibādah,* or who were too ascetic, especially when this went beyond the moderate Islamic position. Islam seeks to create a balance between the needs of the body and those of the soul, between the right of man to live life to its full, and the right of the Creator to be worshipped by man; which is also man's raison d'être.

Islam has laid down certain forms of *'ibādah* to purify the human being both spiritually and materially, individually and collectively, thereby establishing a harmonious community in which feelings of brotherhood and solidarity rule, and without hindering man's duty to build culture and civilization. The obligatory duties such as *ṣalāh,*[9] *zakāh,*[10] *ṣiyām*[11] and *ḥajj*[12] are simultaneously personal as well as social forms of *'ibādah.* While performing these obligations, a Muslim is neither cut off from the mainstream of life nor is he alienated from his community. On the contrary, his ties are emotionally and practically strengthened. This is the reason why Islam did not prescribe monasticism, a practice which requires alienation and seclusion, thus preventing man from enjoying the blessings and *al ṭayyibāt*[13] of normal life and from sharing in its development and promotion.

Islam considers the whole earth a field for religious practice; or the

---

8 Reported by Abū Ya'lā in his *Musnad* on the authority of Anas ibn Mālik. Cited by Ibn Kathīr in his interpretation of Qur'an 57:27 namely: "But the monasticism which they themselves invented, We did not prescribe for them."

9 The act of worship in Islam.

10 The obligatory sharing of wealth with the poor and the community at the yearly rate of 2½ percent of appropriated wealth above a certain minimum.

11 Abstaining from dawn to sunset, every day of the month of Ramaḍān, from any eating, drinking, smoking, and sexual intercourse.

12 The fifth pillar of Islam, consisting of (as at note 5 above) acts performed at Makkah al Mukarramah on the ninth and tenth days of Dhū al Ḥijjah, the last month of the lunar year.

13 *al Ṭayyibāt:* "All things good and pure."

very business of religion. Islam also considers work a form of *'ibādah* and a *jihād*[14] when one's intention is genuinely committed to the service of Allah (SWT). As a result, Islam neither approves of the pursuit of spirituality at the expense of materialism nor of the tendency to "purify the soul" by neglecting and punishing the body, which other religions and philosophies prescribe and advocate. This is made very clear in the Qur'ān: "Our Lord! Give us good in this world and good in the hereafter" (2:201), as well as in the following hadith "O, Allah, set right for me my religion which is the safeguard of my affairs; and set right for me the affairs of my [life in this] world wherein is my living; and set right for me my hereafter on which depends my afterlife; and make life for me [a source] of abundance for every good and make my death a source of comfort for me protecting me against every evil;"[15] and: "Your body has a right over you."[16]

Moreover, the Qur'ān disapproves of and rejects the tendency to prohibit *ṭayyibāt* and beautification *zīnah*[17], which Allah *ta'ālā* has provided for his servants. In a verse revealed in Makkah, Allah (SWT) says:

> O Children of Adam! Wear your beautiful apparel at every time and place of prayer. Eat and drink, but waste not by excess, for Allah loves not those who waste.
>
> Say: who has forbidden the beautiful gifts of Allah which He has produced for His servants, and the things clean and pure which He has provided for sustenance? (7:31-32).

In another *surah,* revealed in Madīnah, Allah (SWT) addresses the believers in the same way:

> O you who believe! Make not unlawful the good things which Allah has made lawful for you. But commit no excess, for Allah does not like those given to excess. Eat of the things which Allah has provided you, lawful and good, but fear Allah, in Whom you believe (5:86-88).

These *āyāt*[18] explain to the believers the true Islamic way of enjoying *ṭayyibāt* and of resisting the excessiveness found in other religions. It

---

[14] *Jihād:* Self-exertion in the cause of Allah (SWT) including peaceful as well as violent means.

[15] Reported by *Muslim.*

[16] Authenticated by all authorities.

[17] *Zīnah:* "Thing or act of ornamentation, beautification taken as source of enjoyment."

[18] *Āyah:* (pl. *Āyāt):* "A verse from the Qur'ān; a sign pointing to the Creator."

is reported that the situational context for the revelation of these two *āyāt* was when a group of the Prophet's companions decided to castrate themselves and to roam the land like monks.

Ibn 'Abbās (RA'A)[19] also reported: "A man came upon the Prophet (ṢA'AS) and said, 'O Messenger of Allah, whenever I eat of this meat I [always] have a desire to make love, therefore, I have decided to abstain from eating meat." Consequently the *āyāt* were revealed.[20]

Narrated Anas ibn Mālik (RA'A): "A group of men came to the houses of the wives of the Prophet (ṢA'AS) asking about his *'ibādah,* and when they were informed about that, they considered their *'ibādah* insufficien. One of them said, 'I will offer *ṣalāh* throughout the night forever.' The other said, 'I will do *ṣiyām* throughout the year and will not break my *ṣiyām.'* Allah's Messenger came to them and said, '...By Allah, I am more submissive to Allah and more afraid of him than you; yet I do *ṣiyām* and I break my *ṣiyām,* I sleep and do night *ṣalāh* and I also marry women. So he who does not follow my *sunnah* is not with me [i.e., not one of my followers].' "

The Prophet's *Sunnah* signifies his understanding of the faith and its application; i.e., his duty toward his Lord, himself, his family, and his followers—giving each the due right in a balanced and moderate way.

1. Defects of Religious Extremism

All these warnings against extremism and excessiveness are necessary because of the serious defects inherent in such tendencies. The first defect is that excessiveness is too disagreeable for ordinary human nature to endure or tolerate. Even if a few human beings could put up with excessiveness for a short time, the majority would not be able to do so. Allah's legislation addresses the whole of humanity, not a special group who may have a unique capacity for endurance. This is why the Prophet (ṢA'AS) was once angry with his eminent companion Mu'ādh, because the latter led the people one day in *ṣalāh* and so prolonged it that one of the people went to the Prophet and complained. The Prophet (ṢA'AS) said to Mu'ādh: "O Mu'ādh! Are you putting the people on trial?" and repeated it thrice.[21]

---

[19] *Raḍiyā Allāhu 'Anhu* (or *'Anhum*): "May Allah be pleased with him/her (or with them)". Said whenever a companion of the Prophet is mentioned by name.

[20] Mukhtaṣar Ibn Kathīr, vol. 1, p. 541

[21] Reported by al Bukhārī.

On another occasion he addressed an imām[22] with unusual anger: "Some of you make people dislike good deeds *[salah]*. So whoever among you leads people in *ṣalāh* should keep it short, short because amongst them are the weak, the old, and the one who has business to attend to."[23]

Furthermore, when the Prophet (ṢA'AS) sent Mu'ādh and Abū Mūsā to the Yemen, he gave them the following advice: "Facilitate [matters to people] and do not make [things] difficult. Give good tidings and do not put off [people]. Obey one another and do not differ [amongst yourselves]."[24]

'Umar ibn al Khaṭṭāb (RA'A) also emphasized this by saying: "Do not make Allah hateful to His servants by leading people in *ṣalāh* and so prolonging it that they come to hate what they are doing."

The second defect is that excessiveness is short-lived. Since man's capacity for endurance and perseverance is naturally limited, and since man can easily become bored, he cannot endure any excessive practice for long. Even if he puts up with it for a while he will soon be overcome by fatigue, physically and spiritually, and will eventually give up even the little he can naturally do, or he may even take a different course altogether substituting excessiveness with complete negligence and laxity. I have often met people who were known for their strictness and extremism; then I lost contact with them for a while. When I inquired about them after a period of time, I found out that they had either deviated and taken the opposite extreme, or had, at least, lagged behind like the "hasty one"[25] referred to in the following hadith:

He [the hasty one] neither covers the desired distance nor spares the back [of his means of transport]."[26]

So is the Prophet's guidance embodied in another hadith: "Do those deeds, which you can endure, as Allah will not get tired [of giving rewards] till you get bored and tired [of performing good deeds]...and the most beloved deed to Allah is the one which is done regularly even if it were little."[27]

Said Ibn 'Abbās: "A female attendant of the Prophet (ṢA'AS) used to do

---

[22] Imām: "Community leader in religious as well as in lay matter."

[23] Reported by al Bukhārī.

[24] Authenticated by all authorities.

[25] The "hasty one" is he who has lost the companionship of his fellow travellers because he has caused the beast he was riding to be fatigued.

[26] Reported by al Bazzāz on the authority of Jābir, with a weak *isnād.*

[27] Reported by al Bukhārī, Muslim, Abū Dā'wūd, and al Nasā'ī on the authority of 'Ā'ishah (RA'A).

ṣiyām during the day and spend the whole night in *iqāmah.*[28] The Prophet (ṢA'AS) was informed of this, and he said, 'In every deed [or action] there is a peak of activity followed by lassitude. He who in his lassitude follows my *Sunnah* is on the right path, but he who in his lassitude follows another [guidance] has [erred and] gone astray."][29]

'Abd Allah ibn 'Umar said: "The Messenger of Allah was told of men who were exhausted by *'ibādah.* He said, 'This is the maximum of Islam and peak of its activity. Each maximum has a peak of activity, and each peak of activity is followed by lassitude...he whose lassitude is in tune with the Book [the Qur'ān] and *Sunnah* is on the right path, but he whose lassitude is for disobedience will perish."[30]

How superb is the Prophet's advice to all Muslims not to overburden themselves in *'ibādah* and to be moderate so that they may not be overcome by fatigue and finally fail to continue. He said: "Religion is very easy, and whoever overburdens himself will not be able to continue in that way. Be right [without excessiveness or negligence], near [perfection], and have good tidings [in being rewarded for your deeds]."[31]

The third defect is that excessive practice jeopardizes other rights and obligations. A sage once said in this respect: "Every extravagance is somehow bound to be associated with a lost right."

When the Prophet (ṢA'AS) knew that 'Abd Allah ibn 'Umar was so absorbed in *'ibādah* that he even neglected his duty toward his wife, he said to him: "O 'Abd Allah! Have I not been correctly informed that you do *ṣiyām* daily and offer *'ibādah* throughout the night?" 'Abd Allah replied, "Yes, O Messenger of Allah!" The Prophet (ṢA'AS) then said: "Don't do that, but do *ṣiyām* and then break your *ṣiyām,* offer *'ibādah* during the night but also sleep. Your body has a right on you, your wife has a right on you, and your guest has a right on you..."[32]

The incident between Salmān al Fārisī (RA'A), the eminent companion, and his devout friend Abū al Dardā' (RA'A) is another case in point. The Prophet (ṢA'AS) made a bond of brotherhood between Salmān and Abū al Dardā'. Once Salmān paid a visit to Abū al Dardā' and found Umm al Dardā' (his wife) dressed in shabby clothes. He asked her why she was in that state, and she replied, "Your brother Abū al Dardā' is

---

[28] *Iqāmah:* "The inception of *ṣalāh* or any other ritual or *'ibādah.*"

[29] Reported by al Bazzāz.

[30] Reported by Aḥmad, and authenticated by Abū Shakir.

[31] Reported by al Bukhārī and al Nasā'ī on the authority of Abū Hurayrah. Explained by al Manāwī.

[32] Reported by al Bukhārī.

not interested in [the *ṭayyibāt* of] this world." In the meanwhile Abū al Dardā' arrived and prepared a meal for Salmān who requested Abū al Dardā' to eat with him, but the latter replied: "I am doing *ṣiyām*." Salmān then said: "I am not going to eat unless you do." So Abū al Dardā' ate [with Salmān]. When it was nighttime Abū al Dardā' got up to offer *'iqāmah*, but Salmān told him to go back to sleep, and so he did. Again Abū al Dardā' got up and once again Salmān told him to go back to sleep. Toward the end of the night, Salmān told Abū al Dardā' to get up, and both offered *ṣalāh*. Salmān then told Abū al Dardā': "Your Lord has a right on you, your self has a right on you, your family has a right on you. So give each the due right." Abū al Dardā' narrated this to the Prophet (ṢA'AS) who said: "Salmān has spoken the truth."[33]

2. The Concept of Religious Extremism

A correct expose and definition of—and an insight into—extremism is the first step toward outlining the remedy. There is no value for any judgment or exposition not based on genuine Islamic concepts and the Sharī'ah, but on mere personal opinions of individuals. The Qur'ān says in this respect: "If you differ on anything among yourselves, refer it to Allah and His Messenger, if you do believe in Allah and the Last Day" (4:59). Throughout the history of the Ummah there has always been an *ijmā';*[34] Referring differences between Muslims to Allah (SWT) and to His Messenger means referring them to His Book, the Qur'ān, and to the *Sunnah* of the Prophet (ṢA'AS). Without such authentication based on Sharī'ah, the Muslim youth—who are accused of "extremism"—will never pay any attention to the *fatāwā*[35] of this or that Muslim scholar, and will deny and refuse to accept such accusation. Furthermore, they will themselves accuse others of ignorance and of falsification.

It is reported that al Imām Muḥammad ibn Idrīs al Shāfi'ī was accused of being a *rāfiḍī*.[36] Outraged by such a cheap accusation, he defiant-

---

[33] Reported by al Bukhārī and al Tirmidhī.

[34] *Ijmā':* "Consensus as a source of Islamic law."

[35] *Fatwā* (pl. *Fatāwā*): "A juristic opinion given by an *'ālim* (hence muftī) on any matter pertinent to Islamic law."

[36] *Rāfiḍī:* "Rejectionist": a person who loves the Prophet (ṢA'AS) and the household of 'Ali ibn Abi Ṭalib but does not accept the caliphate of Abū Bakr and 'Umar. An extremist Shī'ī position.

ly read a verse of poetry which is paraphrased as follows: "If love for all *ahl al bayt*[37] is rejectionism, let the humans and the *jinn* bear witness that I am a rejectionist."

A present-day Muslim *dā'iyah* said, on hearing that he had been branded a reactionary: "If adherence to the Qur'ān and *Sunnah* is reactionism, I wish to live, die, and be resurrected as a reactionary."

In fact it is very important to define accurately such common terms as "reactionism," "rigidity," "extremism" "bigotry," etc., so that they may not constitute ambiguous concepts which can be hurled randomly by one group of people against another, or be interpreted differently by various intellectual and social forces whether on the extreme right or left. Failure to define and comprehend "religious extremism" and to leave the issue to the whimsical desires of people will lead to discord among Muslims. The Qur'ān says:

> If the Truth had been in accord with their desires, truly the heavens and the earth and all the beings therein would have been in confusion and corruption! (23:71).

I would like at this point to draw attention to two important observations. First: The degree of a person's piety as well as that of the society in which he lives affect his judgment of others as far as extremism, moderation, and laxity are concerned. A religious society usually produces a person sensitively aversive to any deviation or negligence, however slight it may be. Judging by the criteria of his own practice and background, such a person would be surprised to find that there are Muslims who do not offer *'ibādah* during the night or practice *ṣiyām*. This is historically obvious. When examining the deeds and practices of people, the nearer one gets to the time of the Prophet (ṢA'AS), his companions and the *Tābi'ūn*,[38] the less worthy seem the deeds and practices of the pious among the later generations. Hence the gist of the saying: "The merits of those nearest to Allah are but the demerits of the righteous."

This reminds one of what Anas ibn Mālik (RA'A) used to tell the *Tābi'ūn* of his contemporaries, "You do things you consider trifling. But during the time of the Prophet (ṢA'AS) these same actions were seen as mortal sins."

The same attitude was expressed by 'Ā'ishah (RA'A), who used to recite

---

[37] The family of the Prophet (ṢA'AS).

[38] *Al Tābi'ī* (pl. *al Tabi'ūn*): "Literally the follower; a member of the first generation of Muslims to follow the contemporaries of the Prophet (ṢA'AS)."

a line of verse by Labīd Ibn Rabī'ah, the well-known poet, which laments the disappearance of those people who provided exemplary patterns of righteous living, thus leaving people to the mercy of the stragglers, whose company is as contagious as a scabby animal. Moreover, she always wondered how Labīd would have felt had he lived to witness the practices of a later generation. 'Ā'ishah's nephew, 'Urwah ibn al Zubayr, also used to recite the same line of verse and wonder how both 'Ā'ishah and Labīd would have felt had they lived in his own age.

On the other hand, a person whose knowledge of and commitment to Islam is little, or who has been brought up in an environment which practices what Allah (SWT) has forbidden and neglects Sharī'ah, will certainly consider even minimal adherence to Islam a kind of extremism. Such a person—who quite often feigns godliness—would not only question and criticize, but would even deny the validity of a certain practice. He would also accuse those who are committed to Islam, and initiate arguments on what is *ḥarām*[39] and what is *ḥalāl.*[40] His attitude would, of course, depend on his distance from the fundamentals of Islam.

Some Muslims—those who are influenced by alien ideologies and practices—consider adherence to clear-cut Islamic teachings concerning eating, drinking, beautification, or the call for the application of Sharī'ah and the establishment of an Islamic state as manifestations of "religious extremism." For such a person, a young Muslim with a beard or a young girl wearing *ḥijāb*[41] are both extremists! Even the commanding of the common good and the prohibition of evil are regarded as forms of extremisim and interference with personal freedom.

Although a basis of faith in Islam is to believe that our religion is right and that those who do not believe in it are wrong, there are Muslims who object to considering those who take a religion other than Islam as *kuffār,*[42] considering this as extremism and bigotry. This is an issue upon which we must never compromise.

Second: It is unfair to accuse a person of "religious extremism" simply because he has adopted a "hard-line" juristic opinion of certain

---

[39] *Ḥarām:* "That which Allah (SWT) has explicitly forbidden humans to do and for which He specified a penalty. The law or deed which is prohibited . (pl. *Muḥarramāt).*"

[40] *Ḥalāl:* "That which Allah (SWT) has explicitly permitted."

[41] *Ḥijāb:* The covering of a Muslim woman; the Islamic style of dress for women.

[42] *Kuffar* or *Kafirūn* (pl. of *Kāfir)* The person quilty of declaring solemnly his/her disbelief"; to say solemnly that Allah (SWT) is not God, or is not the subject of each of His attributes, or that Muḥammad (ṢA'AS) is not His Prophet, or that anything in the Qur'ān is not verbatim truth or revelation from Allah (SWT)."

fuqahā'.[43] If a person is convinced that his opinion is right and that he is bound by it according to Sharī'ah, he is free to do so even if others think that the juristic evidence is weak. He is only responsible for what he thinks and believes even if, in so doing, he overburdens himself, especially since he is not content with only limiting himself to the categorical obligations required of him but seeks Allah's pleasure through supererogatory performances.

People naturally differ on these matters. Some take things easy and facilitate matters, others do not. This is also true of the Prophet's companions. Ibn 'Abbās, for instance, facilitated religious matters, while Ibn 'Umar was strict. In view of all this, it would be enough for a Muslim to support his conviction with evidence from one of the Islamic *madhāhib*,[44] or with a reliable ijtihād,[45] based on sound evidence from the Qur'an or Sunnah. Therefore, should a person be labeled an extremist because he adopts a law derived by one of the four great jurists of Islam—al Shāfi'ī, Abū Ḥanīfah, Mālik, and Aḥmad ibn Ḥanbal—and commits himself to it because he differs from that which various scholars—especially the contemporary—expound? Do we have any right to suppress another person's choice of ijtihād, especially if it relates only to his personal life and behavior?

A great number of Muslim jurists contend that a woman should wear a dress that covers the whole of her body with the exception of her face and hands. The exception of the hands and face is based upon this Qur'ānic verse: "...that they should not display their beauty and ornaments except what [must ordinarily] appear thereof" (24:31). They further emphasize this by supporting it with *aḥādīth*, events, and traditions. Many contemporary *'ulamā'*, including myself, favor this verdict.

On the other hand, a number of eminent Muslim *'ulamā'* argue that both the face and the hands are *'awrah*[46] and must be covered. They cite evidence from the Qur'ān, hadith literature, and established traditions. This argument is advocated by many contemporary *'ulamā'*, especially in Pakistan, India, Saudi Arabia, and the Gulf states. They call upon every Muslim woman who believes in Allah (SWT) and the hereafter to veil her face and wear gloves. If a woman believes in this, and con-

---

[43] *Faqīh* (pl. *Fuqahā'*): Synonymous with *'Ālim*.

[44] *Madhhab* (pl. *Madhāhib*): One of the schools of Islamic law.

[45] *Ijtihād:* "Creative self-exertion to derive laws from the legitimate sources."

[46] *'Awrah:* (literally that part of the body which must be covered): "...the parts of the human body which Sharī'ah requires to be covered in front of other people, those of the same as well as of the opposite sex."

siders it part of the teachings of Islam, should she be branded an extremist? If a man persuades his daughter or his wife to abide by this, should he also be looked upon as an extremist? Do we have the right to force anyone to abandon what he/she believes to be Allah's injunction? Are we not, in this way, asking him/her to seek the anger of Allah (SWT) in order to satisfy our whims and in order to avoid being accused of "extremism"?

The same could also be said of those who adhere to hard-line opinions pertaining to singing, music, drawing, photography, etc. These opinions do not only differ from my own personal ijtihād in these matters but also from the ijtihād of many renowned *'ulamā'.* However, such opinions remain in tune with the views of a number of early and contemporary *'ulamā'.*

However, much of what we criticize in those whom we brand "extremists," such as wearing a short *thawb*[47] instead of a shirt and trousers, or refusing to shake hands with women, which may be considered "excessive," finds its evidence in *uṣūl al fiqh*[48] and the traditions of the Ummah. In that capacity they have been accepted, advocated, and propagated by some of our contemporary *'ulamā'.* Consequently, some devout young Muslims have responded to this in the hope of Allah's mercy and in fear of His punishment. We should not, therefore, condemn the practice of any Muslim or accuse him of "extremism" if he adopts a hard-line opinion based on juristic judgement through which he seeks Allah's pleasure. We have no right to force him to abandon his opinion or ask him to follow a line of behavior which is contrary to his convictions. Our duty is to appeal to him with wisdom, argue with him patiently and nicely, and try to convince him by citing evidence in the hope that he may change his mind and accept what we believe to be the truth.

---

47 A loose outer covering for the body.

48 *Uṣūl al fiqh:* "The sources of Islamic law." *Uṣūl al fiqh:* "Science of Islamic jurisprudence, or the methodology of deriving laws from the sources of Islam and of establishing their juristic or constitutional validity."

3. Manifestations of Extremism

The **first** indications of extremism include bigotry and intolerance, which make a person obstinately devoted to his own opinions and prejudices, as well as rigidity, which deprives him of clarity of vision regarding the interests of other human beings, the purposes of Sharī'ah, or the circumstances of the age. Such a person does not allow any opportunity for dialogue with others so that he may compare his opinion with theirs, and chooses to follow what appears to him most sound. We equally condemn this person's attempt to suppress and discard the opinions of others, just as we condemn the similar attitude of his accusers and opponents. Indeed, we emphatically condemn his attitude if he claims that he alone is right and everybody else is wrong, accusing those who have different ideas and opinions of ignorance and self-interest, and those with different behaviour of disobediance and *fisq,*[49] as if he were an infallible prophet and his words were divinely revealed. This attitude contradicts the consensus of the Ummah, that what every person says can be totally or partly accepted or rejected, except, of course, the *aḥādīth* of Prophet Muḥammad (ṢA'AS).

Strangely, though some of these people take liberty in exercising ijtihād in the most complicated matters and issues and pass notional and whimsical judgments yet they would deprive the contemporary expert *'ulamā'*– singly or collectively – of the right to exercise ijtihād regarding statements which contradict theirs. Some of them never hesitate to give ridiculous opinions on, and interpretations of, the Qur'ān and Sunnah; opinions which are contradictory to those handed down to us by our forefathers, or subsequently arrived at by contemporary *'ulamā'.* This indifference is due to their presumption to be on an equal footing with Abū Bakr, 'Umar, 'Alī, and Ibn 'Abbās (RA'A). This presumption might be less grave if these people admitt that their contemporaries who uphold different views or approaches are also capable of ijtihād like themselve; but they would not.

Bigotry is the clearest evidence of extremisim. An extremist seems to address people in this way: "I have the right to speak, your duty is to listen. I have the right to lead, your duty is to follow. My opinion is right, it cannot be wrong. Your opinion is wrong, it can never be right."

Thus, a bigot can never come to terms with others. Agreement is possi-

---

[49] *Fasaqa* (adj. *Fāsiq):* "To commit a sin, to follow a course of sinfulness and evil, short of apostasy or blasphemy."

ble and can be reached when people hold moderate positions, but a bigot neither knows nor believes in moderation. He stands in relation to people as the East stand in relation to the West—the nearer you get to one, the further you move away from the other.

The issue becomes even more critical when such a person develops the tendency to coerce others, not necessarily physically but by accusing them of *bid'ah,*[50] laxity, *kufr,* and deviation. Such intellectual terrorism is as terrifying as physical terrorism.

The **second** characteristic of extremism manifests itself in a perpetual commitment to excessiveness, and in attempts to force others to do likewise, despite the existence of good reasons for facilitation and the fact that Allah (SWT) has not ordained it. A person motivated by piety and caution may, if he so wishes, choose a hard-line opinion in some matters and on certain occasions. But this should not become so habitual that he rejects facilitation when he needs it. Such an attitude is not in keeping with the teachings of the Qur'ān or Sunnah as is clear from the following verse: "Allah intends every facility for you; He does not want to put you to difficulties" (2:185).

The Prophet (ṢA'AS) also said in a ḥadīth already quoted: "Facilitate [matters to people] and do not make [things] difficult."[51]

He also said: "Allah loves that His dispensations [to make things easier] be accepted, as He dislikes [to see people] committing disobedience."[52]

It is also reported that "whenever the Prophet (ṢA'AS) was given a choice between two options, he always chose the easiest unless it was a sin."[53]

Complicating matters for people and causing constraint in their lives are contrary to the most outstanding qualities of the Prophet Muḥammad (ṢA'AS). These qualities have been mentioned in earlier scriptures and later revealed in the Qur'ān:

> . . . He [Muhammad] allows them as lawful what is good [and pure] and prohibits them from what is bad [and impure], he releases them from their heavy burdens and from the yokes that are upon them (7:157).

This is why the Prophet (ṢA'AS) used to prolong his *ṣalāh* only when

---

[50] *Bid'ah:* "Condemned innovation."

[51] Authenticated by all authorities.

[52] Reported by al Imām Aḥmad and al Bayhaqī on the authority of Ibn 'Umar, and by al Ṭabarī on the authority of Ibn 'Abbās.

[53] Reported by al Bukhārī and al Tirmidhī.

he was alone. In fact, he used to offer *ṣalāh* throughout the night until his feet were swollen. But when leading people in *ṣalāh,* he used to shorten it, taking into consideration the circumstances of his followers and their varying levels of endurance.

He said in this respect, "If any of you leads people in *ṣalāh,* he should shorten it, for among them are the weak, the sick, and the old; and if any of you offers *ṣalāh* alone, then he may prolong [it] as much as he wishes."[54]

Abū Mas'ūd al Anṣarī narrated that a man said to the Prophet (ṢA'AS): "O, Messenger of Allah, I keep away from *ṣalāt al fajr*[55] only because so and so prolongs it." The Prophet (ṢA'AS) became very angry and said: "O, people, some of you make people dislike good deeds *[in this case ṣalah].* Whoever leads people in *ṣalāh* should shorten it because among them are the weak, the old, and those who have business to attend to."[56]

As we have already mentioned, the Prophet (ṢA'AS) reacted in the same way when a man complained to him that Mu'adh (RA'A) prolonged the *ṣalāh.*[57]

Anas Ibn Mālik narrated: "The Prophet (ṢA'AS) said: "When I stand for *ṣalāh,* I intend to prolong it, but I cut it short on hearing the cries of a child, because I do not like to trouble the mother."

It is also strict, excessive and overburdening to require people to observe supererogatories in the same way as they would observe the obligatories, or hold them accountable for the things which are *makrūhāt*[58] as if these were *muḥarramāt.* In fact, we should demand that people observe only what Allah (SWT) has categorically commanded. The extra and additional forms of *'ibādah* are optional.

The following incident shows that this was also the Prophet's opinion. A bedouin once asked the Prophet (ṢA'AS) about the obligatory prescriptions required of him. The Prophet (ṢA'AS) mentioned only three: *ṣalāh, zakāh,* and *ṣiyām.* When the bedouin asked if there was anything else which he must do, the Prophet (ṢA'AS) replied in the negative, adding that the bedouin could volunteer to do more if he so wished. As the bedouin was leaving, he swore never to increase or decrease what the Prophet (ṢA'AS) had asked him to do. When the Prophet (ṢA'AS)

---

54 Reported by al Bukhārī.

55 One of the five daily *ṣalawāt.* It is performed before dawn.

56 Reported by al Bukhārī.

57 See above page 6.

58 *Makrūh* (pl. *Makrūhāt):* "The law or deed which is condemned and discouraged."

heard this he said, "If he is saying the truth, he will succeed"[59] or [said] "he will be granted *jannah.*[60]

If a Muslim in this age observes the *wājibāt*[61] and eschews the most heinous of the *muḥarramāt,* he should be accommodated in the fold of Islam and regarded as one of its advocates so long as his loyalty is to Allah (SWT) and His Messenger (ṢA'AS). Even if he commits some minor *muḥarramāt,* the merits gained by his observance of the five daily *ṣalawāt, ṣalāt al jumu'ah* (Friday prayers), *ṣiyām,* etc. will expiate his small faults.

The Qur'ān says: "Good deeds remove those that are evil" (11:114), and in another verse:

> If you [but] eschew the most heinous of the things which are forbidden, We shall expel out of you all the evil in you and admit you to a state of great honor (4:31).

In view of the above evidence from the Qur'an and *Sunnah,* how could we expel a Muslim from the fold of Islam merely because of his commitment to certain controversial matters which we are not sure are *ḥalāl* or *ḥarām,* or because of his failure to observe something which we are not certain is *wājib* or *mandūb?*[62] This is why I object to the tendency of some pious people to adopt and cling to hard-line opinions, not only in their own personal practice but also in influencing others to do the same. I also object to the charges leveled by such people against any Muslim *'ālim* who disagrees with their line of thought and opts for facilitation in the light of the Qur'ān and Sunnah in order to relieve people of distress and undue restrictions in their religious practice.

The **third** characteristic of extremism is the out-of-time and out-of-place religious excessiveness and overburdening of others, i.e., when applying Islamic principles to people in non-Muslim countries or to people who have only recently converted to Islam, as well as to newly committed Muslims. With all these, emphasis should not be put on either minor or controversial issues, but on fundamentals. Endeavors should be made to correct their concepts and understanding of Islam before anything else. Once the correct beliefs are firmly established, then one can begin to explain the five pillars of Islam and gradually to emphasize

---

[59] *Jannah:* "The Garden, paradise; the eternal abode of the meritorious humans who have been granted the reward of Allah (SWT) on the Day of Judgment."

[60] Reported by al Bukhārī.

[61] *Wājib* (pl. *Wājibāt):* "The law or deed which is obligatory."

[62] *Mandūb* (pl. *Mandūbāt):* "The law or deed which is recommended and expected."

those aspects which make a Muslim's belief and practice compatible, and his entire life an embodiment of what is pleasing to Allah (SWT).

This fact was recognized by the Prophet Muḥammad (ṢA'AS) himself when he sent Mu'ādh (RA'A) to Yemen. He told him:

> You are going to [meet] people of a [divine] scripture, and when you reach them call them to witness that there is no god but Allah and that Muḥammad is His Messenger. And if they obey you in that, then tell them that Allah has enjoined on them five *ṣalawāt* to be performed every day and night. And if they obey you in that, then tell them that Allah has enjoined upon them *ṣadaqah [zakāh]* to be taken from the rich amongst them and given to the poor amongst them.[63]

Notice the gradation in the Prophet's advice to Mu'ādh (RA'A).

I was shocked and dismayed during a tour of North America to find that devout young Muslims—who belong to some Muslim groups—have initiated a great controversy because Muslims sit on chairs during the Saturday and Sunday lectures in mosques instead of sitting on mats on the ground, and do not face the Ka'bah as Muslims do and also because those who attend wear shirts and trousers rather than loose outer coverings, and sit at dining tables to eat rather than on the ground. I was angered by this kind of thinking and behavior in the heart of North America. I, therefore, addressed these people:

> It would be more worthwhile in this materialistic society to make your paramount concern the call to monotheism and the *'ibādah* of Allah (SWT), to remind people of the hereafter, of the noble Islamic values, and to warn them of the heinous acts in which the materially-developed countries have been totally immersed. The norms of behavior and the ameliorations in religious practice are governed by time as well as place, and should be introduced only after the most necessary and fundamental tenets have been firmly established.

In another Islamic center, people were creating a considerable fuss over the showing of a historical or educational film in a mosque, claiming that "mosques have been turned into movie theaters," but forgetting that the purpose of the mosque is to serve the wordly as well as spiritual interest of Muslims. During the time of Prophet Muḥammad (ṢA'AS) the *masjid*—or the mosque—was the center of *da'wah* and of the state,

---

[63] Authenticated by all authorities.

as well as of social activities. We are all aware of the Prophet's granting permission to a group of people from Abyssinia to sport with their spears in the middle of his *masjid,* and that he allowed 'Ā'ishah (RA'A) to watch them.[64]

The **fourth** characteristic of extremism manifests itself in harshness in the treatment of people, roughness in the manner of approach, and crudeness in calling people to Islam, all of which are contrary to the teachings of the Qur'ān and Sunnah.

Allah (SWT) commands us to call to Islam and to His teachings with wisdom, not with foolishness, with amicability, not with harsh words:

> Invite [all] to the Way of your Lord with wisdom and beautiful preaching, and argue with them in ways that are best and most gracious (16:125).

It also describes the Prophet (ṢA'AS), thus:

> Now has come unto you a Messenger from among yourselves. It grieves him that you should perish, ardently anxious is he over you. To the believers he is kind and merciful (9:128).

The Qur'ān also addressed the Prophet (ṢA'AS), defining his relationship with his companions:

> It is part of the mercy of Allah that you [Muḥammad] deal justly with them. If you were severe and harsh-hearted they would have broken away from about you (3:159).

Firmness and harsh-heartedness are mentioned only in connection with two issues in the Qur'ān. First, in connection with war, when a successful military strategy necessitates fortitude and the shelving of leniency until the war comes to an end. "Fight the unbelievers who gird you about and let them find firmness in you" (9:123).

Second, in connection with the execution of punishment on the guilty in accordance with Sharī'ah, there is no room for compassion in applying Allah's injunctions:

> The man and woman guilty of adultery or fornication, flog each of them with a hundred stripes: Let not compassion move you in their case, in a manner prescribed by Allah, if you believe in Allah and the Last Day (24:2).

But in the field of *da'wah,* there is no place for violence and harshness.

---

[64] Reported by al Bukhārī and others.

This is evidenced in the following *aḥādīth:* "Allah loves kindess in all matters"[65] and, "Kindness makes things beautiful, violence makes them defective," as well as in the following wisdom of our forebears: "Whoever desires to command the common good, let him do it gently."

Violence can do nothing more than distort *da'wah* to the path of Allah (SWT). *Da'wah* seeks to penetrate the innermost recesses of man to transform him into a godly person in his conceptions, emotions, and behavior by altering his thoughts, feelings, and will as well as the whole of his being, thereby shaping him into a different person. It also shakes up the structure of the society and alters its inherited beliefs, well-established traditions, moral conventions, and prevailing systems.

All this cannot be achieved without wisdom and amicability, and without taking into consideration human nature—man's obstinancy, resistance to change, and argumentativeness. These characteristics necessitate the exercise of kindness and gentleness when attempting to reach man's heart and mind so that his hardness can be softened, his rigidity abated and his pride checked. This approach was described for us in the Qur'ān as having been followed by earlier prophets and sincere believers who called people to the *'ibādah* of Allah (SWT).

Examples can be found in Ibrāhīm's call to his father and people, in Shu'aib's call to his people, in Mūsā's call to Pharaoh, in the Believer's call to Pharaoh's people, in the Believer's call—in *Sūrat Yāsīn* (36:20)—as well as in the calls of others who directed people to the truth and righteousness.

Let us listen to and contemplate the spirit in which the Believer—a man who possesses *'īmān* from among Pharaoh's people—addresses Pharaoh and the people expressing his sense of belonging to them and his concern for their destiny and for the permanence of their dominion and glory:

> O my People! Yours is the dominion this day: You have the upper hand in the land: but who will help us from the punishment of Allah should it fall upon us? (40:29).

Then he reminds them of earlier nations who refused to listen to the message of Allah (SWT):

> O my People! Truly I do fear for you something like the Day [of disaster] of the Confederates [in sin]—Something like the fate of the people of Nūḥ, and 'Ād and Thamūd, and those

---

[65] Reported by al Bukhārī.

> who came after them: but Allah never wishes injustice upon His servants. (40:30-31).

Then he describes the disaster which might befall them on the Day of Judgment, a day which they believe in, one way or another:

> And O my People! I fear for you a Day when there will be mutual calling [and wailing], a Day when you will turn your backs and flee: no defender shall you have from Allah. Any whom Allah leaves to stray, there is none to guide (40:32-33).

He continues his earnest beseeching in a manner dominated by gentleness and compassion; he warns, but he also inspires with hope:

> O my People! Follow me! I will lead you to the Right Path. O my People! This life of the present is nothing but [temporary] convenience. It is the hereafter that is the home that will last... And O my People! How [strange] it is for me to call you to salvation while you call me to the Fire. You do call upon me to blaspheme against Allah and to join with Him partners of whom I have no knowledge, and I call you to the Exalted in Power, Who forgives again and again! (40:38-42).

Then he ends his advice with the following:

> Soon will you remember what I say to you [now]. My [own] affair I commit to Allah, for Allah [ever] watches over His servants (40:44).

This is the approach and manner which contemporary Muslim *du'āh* should emulate and adopt with the stubborn, and with people of other religions.

This is also embodied in Allah's advice to His two messengers, Mūsā ('AS)[66] and his brother Hārūn ('AS), who were sent to preach to Pharaoh:

> Go, both of you, to Pharaoh, for he has indeed transgressed all bounds. But speak to him mildly, perchance he may take warning or fear [Allah]. (20:43-44).

Accordingly. Mūsā ('AS) addressed Pharaoh very gently:

> Would you that thou should be purified [from sin]. And that

---

66 *'Alayhi al salām* or *'Alayhim al salām (pl.):* "Upon him [or them] be the blessing [of Allah (SWT)]." Said whenever a prophet other than Muḥammad (ṢA'AS) is mentioned by name.

I guide you to your Lord, so that you should fear Him? (79:18-19).

No wonder then that experienced people in *da'wah* reject and disapprove of the young peoples' manner in arguing with those who hold different opinions! Rather than calling people to the Way of Allah (SWT) with wisdom, they are quite often harsh, rough, and crude. No distinction is made between the old and the young; no special consideration is given to those whose age or status deserves special respect, that is, parents, teachers, the learned, or those who have precedence in *da'wah* and *jihād.* Nor do the young people differentiate between those sectors in the community—such as the laity, the illiterate, and the misled—who are ceaselessly battling to earn a living, and those who actively resist Islam out of malice or treason, not ignorance.

Such lack of insight is still dominant in Muslim society, despite the fact that the early scholars of *aḥādīth* literature distinguished very clearly between the common innovators who did not call others to their innovation and those who deliberately publicized and defended their *bid'ah* (condemed innovations). The reports of the former were accepted, while those of the latter were rejected.

Suspicion and distrust are also manifestations of extremisim. An extremist readily accuses people and quickly passes judgement contrary to the generally accepted norm: "innocent until proven guilty." He considers a person guilty the moment he suspects him of something. He jumps to conclusions rather than looking for explanations. The slightest mistake is blown out of all proportions; a mistake becomes a sin, and a sin *kufr.* Such a reaction is a stark violation of the spirit and teachings of Islam which encourage Muslims to think well of other Muslims, to try to find an excuse for their misbehavior, and to help them improve their words and deeds.

The religious sincerity and integrity of those who disagree with such an extremist are always called into question. An extremist would depict people as being guilty of transgression, innovation, or disrespect for the Prophet's Sunnah even if their views are solidly based upon authentic Islamic texts.

One could cite many examples: If you argue that carrying a stick or eating while sitting on the ground has nothing to do with the Sunnah, you would be accused of disrespect for the Prophet (ṢA'AS) himself. Not even learned Muslim scholars and *'ulamā'* are spared such accusations. If a *faqīh* gives a *fatwā* which facilitates matters for Muslims, he is considered lax on religious issues; if a Muslim *dā'īyah* tries to call to Islam in a manner suitable to the spirit and the taste of the age, he is accused of succumbing to and patronizing Western civilization.

Moreover, these accusations are not only hurled at the living but also at the dead, who are unable to defend themselves. No one holding a different opinion can escape unjust indiscriminate accusations, such as being a Freemason, a predeterminist, a Jahmī, or a rationalist Mu'tazilī. Even the four great jurists of Islam who established the main Islamic juristic schools and who have earned the respect of the majority of Muslims throughout the centuries have not escaped the venomous slander of the extremists. Indeed, the whole history of the Muslim Ummah after the fourth century AH, with its glorious legacy and unprecedented civilization, has been a target of unjustified criticism. It is considered by the extremists as being the source of contemporary evils, the roots of our malaise. To some extremists, it was a period of conflict and discord, of struggle for personal power; for others, a period of ignorance and even *kufr.*

This destructive tendency is not new. Extremists existed even during the time of the Prophet (ṢA'AS). Once, an extremist among the *Anṣār* (the Muslims of Madīnah) accused the Prophet (ṢA'AS) of favoritism in his divison and distribution of the spoils of war.

The gravest shortcoming of the contemporary extremists is suspicion. Had they understood and comprehended the Qur'ān and Sunnah, they would have discovered that both seek to foster in the mind of each and every Muslim the confidence and trust of other fellow Muslims.

A Muslim is not even allowed to publicize the minor mistakes and faults of others or become blind to their merits; thus some people are interested in criticizing others and in praising themselves: "Therefore, justify not yourselves: He knows best who it is that guards against evil" (53:32).

Indeed, Islam strongly warns against two characteristics: despairing of Allah's mercy and suspecting fellow human beings. Allah (SWT) says:

> O you who believe! Avoid suspicion as much [as possible]: for suspicion in some cases is a sin (49:12).

The Prophet (ṢA'AS) also says in this respect: "Avoid suspicion, for suspicion is the false element in a talk."[67]

The origins of all this include suspicion as well as arrogance and the despising of other people. These are the basis of the first act of disobedience—that of Satan; he refused Allah's command for him to pro-

[67] Authenticated by all authorities.

strate himself to Ādam, claiming: "I am better than he [is]" (38:76).

It is worthwhile to heed the warning embodied in the following ḥadīth: "If you hear a person saying that people are ruined, he himself will be ruined for being vain and conceited."[68]

And in another narration ". . .he himself caused their ruin," i.e., by his suspicion and snobbery, and by causing them to despair of Allah's mercy.

Vanity is one of the human traits which causes degeneration and which our Muslim scholars call the "sins of the hearts." The Prophet (ṢA'AS) warned us against these sins: "There are three deadly sins – unrestrained avarice, desire, and vanity." A true Muslim never takes pride in his work or actions, since he is never sure that Allah (SWT) will accept them.

The Qur'ān describes the charitable people: "And those who dispense their charity with their hearts full of fear, because they will return to their Lord" (23:60). It is reported in hadith literature that this Qur'ānic verse is about people who do righteous deeds but fear that Allah (SWT) may not accept them. Ibn 'Aṭā' said: "Allah may open up for you the gates of obedience, but He may not open up for you the gates of acceptance. He may ordain you a state of disobedience which may happen to lead you to the right path. The disobedience which teaches you humility is better than the piety which vests you with vanity and arrogance!"

This derives from the following saying by 'Alī ibn Abū Ṭālib (RA'A): "A mishap that befalls a person is better in the sight of Allah than a good action which initiates pride."

Ibn Mas'ūd also said: "Ruin is caused by two traits – pride and despair. Happiness cannot be attained without effort and stuggle. A vain person does not make any effort because he believes that he is perfect; a despairing person does not make any effort because he believes it is useless."

Extremism reaches its utmost limit when a single group deprives all people of the right to safety and protection, and instead sanctions their killing and the confiscation of their lives and property. This, of course, occurs when an extremist holds all people – except those in his group – to be *kuffār.* This kind of extremism severs any bond between such a person and the rest of the Ummah. This is the trap into which the Khawārij fell during the dawn of Islam, although they were known for their strict observance of religious duties such as *ṣalāh, ṣiyām,* and recitation of the Qur'ān. However their thinking rather than their conscience was distorted and corrupt. Hence they were so infatuated with their belief

---

68 Reported by Muslim.

and behavior that they, unintentionally, deviated from the right path.

The Prophet (ṢA'AS) described the devotion of such people by saying: "One of you would hold insignificant his own *ṣalāh* compared with their [the Khawārij] *ṣalāh,* and his *qiyām*[69] compared with their *qiyām,* his recitation [of the Qur'ān] compared with their recitation."[70] Nevertheless, he said of them: "They would recite the Qur'ān but it would not go beyond their throat, and they pass through religion without a mark."[71] This means that they would slip out of religion as an arrow would slip out of its bow.

The Prophet (ṢA'AS) also said of them that they regard it as their duty to "destroy adherents of Islam and save the idol-worshippers."[72]

This is why when a Muslim fell into their hands and was asked about his identity, he replied that he was a *mushrik*[73] curious to find out about Allah's message and book. On hearing this the Khawārij told the man that they would protect him and grant him safe passage. In support of their decision, they recited the following verse from the Qur'ān:

> If one amongst the pagans asks you for asylum, grant it to him, so that he may hear the Word of Allah; and then escort him to where he may be secure. That is because they are men without knowledge (9:6).

The irony is that if the man had admitted that he was a Muslim they would have killed him.

Unfortunately, some Muslims have not yet learned this lesson. The *Jamā'at al Takfīr wa al Hijrah* group seems to be following in the footsetps of the Khawārij. They readily brand as *kāfir* anybody who commits a sin and does not immediately repent. More condemned in their view are the rulers who do not apply Sharī'ah, as well as the people who submit to such rulers. Still more sinful in their view are the *'ulamā'* who do not openly condemn both as *kuffār,* as well as those who reject the group's beliefs and submit to the laws elaborated by the four great jurists

---

[69] *Qiyām: "Ibādah* during the night."

[70] Reported by Muslim.

[71] Reported by Muslim.

[72] Reported by Muslim.

[73] *Shirk:* "Association of other beings with Allah (SWT); opposite of *Tawḥīd." Mushrik* (pl. *Mushrikūn):* "The person who practices or believes in *shirk.*"

of Islam on the basis of *ijma', qiyās, maslaḥah mursalah,* or *istiḥsān.*[74] Moreover, any one who first pledges support for their cause and joins their group, then decides to leave it – for one reason or another – is considered a *murtadd*[75] and must be put to death. Indeed, they hold all the Islamic periods succeeding the fourth century A.H. as periods of ignorance and *kufr,* worshipping the idol of tradition rather than Allah (SWT).[76]

In this way, the group became so excessive in accusing people of *kufr* that they spared neither the dead nor the living. The group thus have run into deep trouble, because accusing a Muslim of *kufr* is a very serious matter which entails very serious consequences – his killing and the confiscation of his property become lawful. As a *kāfir,* he must be separated from his wife and children; there can be no bond between him and other Muslims; he must be deprived of his inheritance and cannot be inherited from; he must be denied the Islamic burial and the *ṣalāh* for the dead person; and he must not be buried in a Muslim graveyard.

The Prophet (ṢA'AS) said: "When a Muslim calls another Muslim *kāfir,* then surely one of them is such."[77] This means that unless the accusation is validated and substantiated, it will fall back on the accuser, who will face great danger in this world and in the hereafter.

Usāmah ibn Zayd said: "If a man says, 'I witness that there is no god but Allah,' he has embraced Islam, and [consequently] his life and property should be granted safety. If he said so in fear or to protect himself from the sword, he will account for that before Allah. We should [judge] the apparent."[78]

The Prophet (ṢA'AS) rebuked Usāmah when he discovered that the latter had killed a man who had uttered the *shahādah*[79] following a battle in which the man's tribe was defeated. When Usāmah argued that he thought – at the time – that the man did so as a shelter and in fear, the

---

74 *Qiyās:* "Logical deduction from the Qur'ān and *Sunnah* as sources of Islamic law." *Maṣlaḥah Mursalah:* "Public welfare neither commended nor prohibited in any Islamic source, as a source of Islamic law." *Istiḥsān:* "As a source of Islamic law, the acceptance of a rule because of its superior equity in comparison with an already established law."

75 *Riddah* (adj. *Murtadd):* "Abjuration of allegiance to Allah (SWT) as well as to the Islamic state of which one is a citizen." Apostasy.

76 See 'Abd al Raḥmān Abū al Khayr: *Ḍikrāyātī Ma' Jamā'at al Muslimīn – al Takfīr wa al Ḥijrah.*

77 Reported by al Bukhārī.

78 Reported by al Bukhārī.

79 *Shahādah:* "The act of witnessing that there is no god but Allah and that Muḥammad is His Prophet, Servant and Messenger; the verbal content of that act."

Prophet (ṢA'AS) said: "Did you look into his heart after he had confessed that there is no God but Allah?" Usāmah relates: "He [the Prophet] went on repeating this to me till I wished I had not embraced Islam before that day."

Sharī'ah teaches that those who embrace Islam with certainty of mind can only be expelled from its fold by proven and substantiated evidence. Even major *muḥarramāt* such as murder, fornication, and drinking alcohol do not justify the accusation of *kufr,* provided that the person concerned does not show disrespect for, reject, or refuse to recognize the Sharī'ah.

This is why the Qur'ān established brotherly love between the person who commits a premeditated murder and the next of kin to the murdered as this verse shows:

> And for him who is forgiven somewhat by his [injured] brother, prosecution according to usage and payment unto him in kindness (2:178).[80]

The Prophet (ṢA'AS) also addressed a person who cursed an alcoholic who had already been punished several times for alcoholism: "Do not curse him; he loves Allah and His Messenger."[81]

Further, the Sharī'ah has prescribed different punishments for crimes such as murder, fornication, and drunkeness. Had all of these been *kufr,* then they would have been been punished in accordance with the law of *riddah.*

All the obscure and vague evidence on which the extremists base their accusations are refuted by fundamental and categorical texts in both the Qur'ān and Sunnah. This issue was settled by the Ummah centuries ago—it is futile to try to revive and renew it.

---

[80] Muḥammad Asad's translation.

[81] Reported by al Bukhārī.

CHAPTER TWO

Causes of Extremism

Extremism does not originate haphazardly. It must indeed have causes and motivation. Like living organisms, events and actions do not come out of the blue and cannot germinate without seeds. Rather, they are governed by the law of cause and effect—one of Allah's *sunan*[1]—in His creation. Knowledge of the causes in this respect is essential to enable us to define the remedy which, medically speaking, must always be preceded by diagnosis. But diagnosis is impossible—at least extremely difficult—when causes are not known. With this in mind, we endeavor to examine the causes and the motives which have generated extremism—a term which has become synonymous with *ghulūw,* i.e., excessiveness in religion.

We must realize at the outset that no single cause is wholly responsible for the spread of extremism. It is a complex phenomenon with numerous interrelated causes, some of which are direct, others indirect, some found in the distant past, others in the present. Consequently, we should not focus on one cause and totally ignore the others, as do people who advocate some schools of thought. Psychologists, and especially psychoanalysts, for instance, attribute all behavior to certain subconscious psychological causes. Meanwhile, sociologists point to man's helplessness vis-a-vis social and environmental influences; for them, man is simply a lifeless puppet whose strings are in the hands of society.[2] The advocates of historical materialism emphasize economic forces which, they argue, create events and change the course of history.

On the other hand, others who hold a more comprehensive and balanced view believe that the causes are complex and interrelated, producing various effects which, although differing from one cause to another, have their undeniable impact in the final analysis. It is important that we should not concentrate on one cause of extremism, as its causes are varied and could be direct or indirect, manifest or latent. The causes of extremisim may be religious, political, social, economic, psychological, intellectual, or a combination of all of these. The main cause may be in the extremist

---

[1] *Sunan*: "Laws and patterns in the Universe."

[2] Cf. the works of Emile Durkheim.

himself, in his relationship with the members of his family, or—if deeply analyzed—may be found in his society and all its contradictions between faith and behavior, ideals and reality, religion and politics, words and actions, aspirations and achievements, the secular and the divine. Naturally, if these contradictions are tolerated by the old they, cannot be tolerated by the young. If some young people do tolerate and bear contraditions, they do so only temporarily.

Extremism may also be initated by the corruption of regimes, i.e., the despotism of rulers, their egotistic pursuits, their adherence to the views of corrupt counsellors and advisers as well as various foreign enemies of the Ummah, and their total disregard for the rights of their peoples. These practices have severed the bond between religion and the state.

Undoubtedly, one of the main causes of extremism is a lack of knowledge of—and insight into—the purposes, spirit, and essence of *dīn.*[3] However, such a lack, which does not imply total ignorance, does not lead to extremism or excessiveness, but rather to their opposites, i.e., degeneration and laxity. It implies, however, semi-knowledge. A person may presume—and sometimes genuinely believe—that he knows all there is to know; that he is a scholar, a *faqīh.* But actually he has no more than a hodgepodge of undigested and unassimilated "knowledge" which neither enhances insight nor clarifies vision. A person possessing such "knowledge" concentrates on marginal and trivial issues only, and thereby fails to see the relationship between the parts which form the whole (and the whole itself) or between the categorical and fundamental texts vis-a-vis the allegorical ones. Further, this person cannot synthesize or give preponderance to evidence over mere considerations. Aware of the danger of such semi-knowledge. Abū Isḥāq al Shāṭibī (RA'A)[4] discussed it in his book *al I'tiṣām.* He argued that self-presumption and conceit are the root causes of *bid'ah* as well as the disunity of the Ummah, and could lead to internal schism and gradual disintegration. He asserted that when a person unduly presumes himself or is presumed to be knowledgeable in religious matters and capable of exercising ijtihād, and when he acts accordingly, claiming that he has the right to present different opinions and interpretations, whether the verdicts and opinions pertain to minor aspect or to major aspect of *dīn,* thus he cites major

---

[3] *Al Dīn*: "The normative or perfect religion which Allah (SWT) ordained for humanity, including faith, ethics, law, devotions, institutions, and judgment."

[4] *Raḥmatu Allāhi 'Alayhi* (*'Alayhā* or *'Alayhim*): "May Allah's mercy fall upon him (her or them)." Said whenever the departed Muslim is mentioned by name.

aspects, to pull down major ones; he is indeed a *mubtadi'.* In the following hadith, the Prophet (ṢAAS) warned against such a person:

> Allah does not take away the knowledge by taking it away from [the hearts of] the people, but takes it away when none of the *'ulamā'* remain, and people will take as their leaders ignorant persons who when consulted will give their verdict without knowledge. So they will go astray and will lead the people astray.[5]

Some of the learned infer from the above hadith that people are never led astray by genuine *'ulamā',* but in the absence of the latter people turn to semi-*'ulamā'* who lead them astray by giving incorrect advice. Thus it has been said that a trustworthy person never betrays a trust, but the traitorous one does. We add to this: a genuiune *'ālim* never innovates, but a semi-*'ālim* does.

Anas ibn Mālik (RAA) narrated: "Rabī'ah was once seen weeping bitterly. When he was asked whether a calamity had befallen him, he replied, 'No, but people are seeking *fatwā* from persons who possess no knowledge.'"

The fact is that semi-knowledge, coupled with vanity and pride, is more dangerous and subversive than an admitted total ignorance, because the former is the ignorance of a person who is not aware of his limitations. Such ignorance manifests itself in various ways, the most important of which is sticking rigidly to the literal meanings of the texts in total disregard for their essence and purposes. The phenomenon is not new. Centuries ago the Ẓāhirīyah school of thought did exactly the same. The adherents of this school rejected both *ta'līl al aḥkam*[6] and consequently *qiyās,* because they believed that Sharī'ah differentiates between the identicals and equates the variants.

The contemporary Ẓāhirīyah follows the old one by seeking to regulate acts of *'ibādah* and transactions without any kind of rationalization, reflection or attempt to understand their deeper meanings. Perhaps the only difference between the two schools is that the adherents of the old one were much more committed to their convictions, while their successors never admit that they only blindly stick to the negative attitudes of their predecessors, i.e., total rejection of *ta'līl.* My own opinion, as well as that of other *'ulamā'* who have studied the matter deeply, is that *'ibādah* is the cause and purpose of the obligatory duties which are not, and

---

5 Reported by al Bukhārī.

6 *Ta'līl al aḥkam*: "Rationalization of the legal verdicts in the Shar'iah."

can never be, an object of an assessment. However, the teachings which are aimed to regulate our lives can be, and must be, analyzed.[7]

It is wrong, therefore, to claim that a person who gives money to poor Muslims or finances useful Islamic projects can dispense with *ḥajj;* nor should it be claimed that giving the price value of *hady al tamattu*[8] in *ṣadaqah* or *qirān*[9] during *ḥajj* is better than the actual sacrifice. It is equally inconceivable to say that modern taxes can replace *zakāh,* the third pillar of Islam and one which is on a par with *ṣalāh.* In fact, *ṣalāh* is rarely ever mentioned in the Qur'ān without *zakāh* following immediately, or in the verse that follows after. Nor, of course, should *Ramaḍān* be replaced by another month for *ṣiyām,* nor Friday by another day for ṣalāt *al jum'ah,* which is obligatory for Muslims. But in matters other than the purely devotional ones, we can examine the reasons and take account of the underlying meanings and purposes. Once we grasp those we can base verdicts upon them and either accept or reject them.

Let us examine the following texts:

(a) It is related in an authentic hadith that a Muslim should not carry a copy of the Qur'ān when traveling in the land of the *kuffār* or the enemy. But if we examine the reason underlying this prohibition, we conclude that the Prophet (ṢA'AS) prohibited this out of his concern that the *kuffār* might do harm to or defile *the Book.* In the absence of such harm or defilement, Muslims can take it with them wherever they wish. This is the customary practice among all Muslims today. Indeed, people of other religions and faiths now compete to distribute their "sacred books" and utilize all possible means in the process. Muslims are trying to do the same through translations of the meanings of the Qur'ān for non-Arabic speakers.

(b) Another authentic hadith prohibits a Muslim woman from traveling unless she is accompanied by a *maḥram.*[10] Surely, the main purpose of this prohibition was to protect women at a time when traveling was a laborious and dangerous experience. Presently, however, the means of transportation used by travelers have considerably reduced the risks faced by a woman traveling on her own. Her husband, for instance, can

---

[7] This has been authenticated by evidence from the Qur'ān and *Sunnah* by al Imām al Shāṭibī in his books *Al Muwāfaqāt* and *al I'tiṣām*.

[8] An animal offered as a sacrifice by the pilgrim doing *'umrah* ("the minor *ḥajj*") before *ḥajj* while assuming *iḥrām* ("the pilgrim's dress") separately for both.

[9] Performing *ḥajj* with *'umrah* preceding it while one is keeping the same *iḥrām* for both.

[10] *Maḥram*: "A male relative who, because of kinship ties, is not permitted to marry the woman in question."

take her to the airport and see her off. When she arrives at the other end, a *maḥram* can meet her and convey her safely to her final destination. In fact, the Prophet (ṢA'AS) foresaw such a development, for he said that there would come a time when people could travel from Iraq to the Ka'bah (in Makkah) fearing none except Allah (SWT).

(c) The Prophet (ṢA'AS) also did not permit a Muslim who had been away from his family for a long period of time to arrive back at night. He himself used to return only in the mornings or early evenings. There are two reasons for this. First, arriving home unexpectedly after a long absence may indicate that the husband mistrusts his wife and intends to take her unawares. This kind of mistrust is not acceptable in Islam. Secondly, it is argued that the prohibition seeks to give the wife the right to know of her husband's arrival so that she may beautify herself for him. But in modern times a traveler can come home any time he likes, on the condition that he informs his wife by telephone or by letter, telex, telegram, etc. Further, today's traveler cannot always choose when to travel, for he is governed by schedules and timetables. Therefore, such a prohibition cannot be taken at its face value; it must be analyzed on the basis of its original purpose and intent with regard to the circumstances of time and place.

As previously mentioned, compulsory obligations related to *'ibādah* cannot be rationalized in order to exclude *zakāh* by claiming that it is part of the financial and economic system rather than of *'ibādah. Zakāh,* in addition to being a pillar of Islam —as a religious duty and a divine prescription—constitutes a significant and permanent source of income in Islamic Sharī'ah, and is therefore, a pillar of the Islamic economic system as well. That is why all *madhāhib* apply rational deduction on its *aḥkām* including *qiyās* because of zakah's actual or potential growth like wealth. Personally, I believe that it is obligatory for Muslims to give ten percent (one-tenth) or five percent (half of one-tenth) of all the produce of cultivated lands to the poor, whether fruit or grain, fresh or dry, edible or not. All the necessary reasons are there, i.e., growth, the established right of the needy to the money of the rich as well as to the vegetables of the growers, who need to be purified and sanctified: "Of their goods take alms, that so you might purify and sanctify them" (9:103).

However, a contemporary Ẓāhirī (literalist) rejected the foregoing argument by quoting a hadith which says, "There is no *ṣadaqah* on vegetables."

[11] See al Qaraḍāwī, Y. *Fiqh al Zakāh*, 1:349-358.

He also argued that there is no precedent in the Prophet's practice to show that he took *zakāh* on vegetables. I replied that the first argument is false, for the ḥadīth is weak and is therefore an inconclusive evidence against the overall spirit of the Qur'ān and *Sunnah.* This ḥadīth has not been authenticated by any of the ḥadīth scholars but was only reported by al Tirmidī, who eventually classified it as weak, adding that nothing authentic can be attributed to the Prophet (ṢA'AS) in this respect.

The second argument is also false for two reasons, one of which was put forward by al Imām Ibn al 'Arabī, who said that there was no need for citing this kind of evidence as the issue is categorically dealt with in the Qur'ān: "Eat of their fruit in their seasons, but render the dues that are proper on the day that the harvest is gathered" (6:141). The second reason is that even if there was no precedent in the Prophet's practice, we should deduce that he might have left the matter to the conscience of his followers, since in those days it was difficult to preserve fruits and vegetables.

However, the contemporary Zahirī literalist persisted that there is a ḥadīth which restricts *zakāh* only to dates, raisins, wheat, and barley. But this ḥadīth is also weak. It has not been authenticated by any of the scholars, and it has not, therefore, been taken as evidence by any of the *madhāhib.* Hence, how could it stand as evidence against the comprehensive audmenticated texts which institute *zakāh* as obligatory on all the produce of land as stated in the following Qur'ānic verse:

> It is He who produces gardens with trellises and without dates and tilth with produce of all kinds, and olives and pomegranates, similar [in kind] and different [in variety]. Eat of their fruit in their season, but render the dues that are proper on the day that the harvest is gathered (6:141).

And in another:

> O you who believe! Give of the good things which you have earned, and of the fruits of the earth which We have produced for you...(2:267).

There is also an authentic ḥadīth which makes the rendering of *zakāh* more inclusive than the contemporary literalists would like to admit. The Prophet (ṢA'AS) said: "One-tenth on a land watered by rivers or rain [i.e., easy, natural irrigation]; five percent on a land watered by *sāqiyah* [artificial irrigation]."[12]

---

[12] Abū Bakr ibn al 'Arabī: *Aḥkām al Qur'ān.*

These texts are not confined to a particular produce, and the obligatory rendering of one-tenth—or half of one-tenth—is clearly evident. This was what Abū Ḥanīfah deduced from all the above texts and later accepted by 'Umar ibn 'Abd al 'Aziz. This interpretation is in tune with the essence and purposes of Sharī'ah. May Allah (SWT) bless the Mālikī Imām and just judge Abū Bakr Ibn al 'Arabī, who pointed out that the views of Abū Ḥanīfah regarding this issue are sounder than those put forward by the others. These views were expressed in al 'Arabī's interpretation of the Qur'ānic verse: "It is He who produces gardens..." (6:141)[13] and in his explanation of the aformentioned ḥadīth, "On a land watered by rivers."[14]

After presenting the evidence put forward by different *madhāhib* and showing their weaknesses, Ibn al 'Arabī says in *Aḥkam al Qur'an* 2/947 "Abū Ḥanīfah made the [previously mentioned] verse his mirror [guide] and was consequently able to see the truth." He also says in *Sharḥ al Tirmidhī:*

> With regard to this issue, Abū Ḥanīfah's *madhab* provides the most solid evidence, shows the most provident care for the deprived and gratitude for Allah's bounties, all of which are evident in the general content of the verse and the ḥadīth.

In conclusion, failing to see the relevance between the *aḥkām* and their reasons will lead to dangerous contradictions when we differentiate between the similar ones and equate the variants; this is contrary to the justice which is the basis of Sharī'ah. It is true that psuedoscholars too often indulge in such complex issues seeking (without knowledge or insight) reasons for *aḥkām,* and thus unjustly extend their domain without authentic evidence. This should not hinder our endeavor to give people their due right, or to open the gate of ijtihād for those who are qualified and capable, warning at the same time against intruders and parasites.

---

13 Ibid.

14 Abū Bakr ibn al 'Arabī: *'Ārīḍat al Aḥwadhī fi Sharḥ al Tirmidhī.*

1. Occupation with Side Issues

Intellectual shallowness and lack of religious insight also manifest themselves in an intense interest in marginal issues at the expense of major ones—those which could affect the existence, identity, and destiny of the whole Ummah. There is excessive and unnecessary talk about growing a beard, wearing clothes below the ankle, moving of the finger during reading the *tashāhhud* in prayer, acquisition of photographs and so on. Unfortunately, such time-wasting arguments persist and occupy our thinking at a time when we are being confronted by the unrelenting hostility—and infiltration—of secularism, communism, Zionism, and Christianity, as well as deviationist groups in the Muslim world. Christian missionaries are waging a new crusade against the Ummah with the intent of undermining its historical and Islamic character. Muslims are being mercilessly slaughtered in various parts of the world; Muslim *du'āt* are being subjected to the worst forms of intimidation and aggression.

Strangely—and indeed tragically—I found that those who emigrated to the United States, Canada, and Europe in pursuit of knowledge or to earn a living have actually brought with them such conflict and controversies on marginal issues as are prevalent in their societies. I have often witnessed—or heard about—violent debates and stormy arguments which have succeeded in creating disunity among Muslims on issues that are subject to extrapolation and ijtihād, some of which I have already outlined, and on which jurists will continue to differ and people are unlikely ever to agree. Instead of such futile wrangling, it would be far better for these Muslim expatriates to concentrate their efforts on disseminating true adherence to Islam among themselves, especially among the young, committing them to the obligations, and helping them to avoid major prohibitions. If Muslims in these countries succeeded in accomplishing these things, they would realize a great hope and open up new opportunities for the dissemination of Islam.

It is a pity that those who initiate and encourage these confrontations are well known for their negligence of essential religious duties, i.e., kindness to parents, cautious investigation of what is permissible and what is prohibited, execution of their own tasks, and respect for the rights of their spouse, children, and neighbors. However, instead of improving themselves, they derive great pleasure from initiating conflicts which eventually lead them to take either a hostile or a hypocritical position.

Such wrangling is the subject of the following ḥadīth: "People going astray after guidance are bound to be argument-stricken."[15]

It is also not uncommon to find people warning Muslims not to eat animals slaughtered by the People of the Book (the Christians and Jews) although there are many past and present *fatāwā* which have legitimized this. Yet, if we examine the attitude and behavior of these people with regard to other more serious matters, we find that they engage in some definitely forbidden practices. This reminds me of a man living in the United States who, I was told by trustworthy brothers, spoke in full-throathed clarity against eating the meat of animals slaughtered by Jews or by Christians, yet he did not mind eating with others at the same table while they were drinking alcohol. Nonetheless, he unreservedly takes this extreme stand against uncertain and controversial matters.

Such contradictory behavior of some Muslims once outraged 'Abd Allah ibn 'Umar (RA'A) when a man from Iraq asked him—following the murder of the great Muslim martyr al Ḥusayn ibn 'Alī (RA'A) — whether it was *ḥalāl* or *ḥarām* to kill a mosquito. Aḥmad related in his *musnad:*

> As I was sitting with Ibn 'Umar, a man came and asked him about the blood of a mosquito. (In another version of the ḥadīth, the man asked about a pilgrim killing a mosquito). Ibn 'Umar asked the man: "Where are you from?" The man answered, "From Iraq." Then Ibn 'Umar said: "Look at this man! He is asking me about the blood of mosquitoes when they [the Iraqis] killed the Prophet's grandson (i.e., al Ḥusayn ibn 'Alī (RA'A). I heard the Prophet (SAAS) saying: 'They [al Ḥasan and al Ḥusayn] are my two sweetest-smelling flowers of this world.' "[16]

2. Excessive Extension of Prohibitions

One of the indications of this shallowness, of the lack of a thorough knowledge of Islamic jurisprudence and of Sharī'ah, is making things difficult through an invalid extension of prohibitions despite the very clear warnings against this in the Qur'ān and Sunnah:

> But say not—for any false thing that your tongues may put

[15] Reported by Aḥmad, Abū Dāwūd, and al Tirmidī.

[16] Reported by Aḥmad. Al Shaykh Aḥmad Shākir confirms that its *isnād* is authentic.

forth: "This is lawful and this is forbidden," so as to ascribe false things to Allah. For those who ascribe false things to Allah will never prosper (16:116).

The Prophet's companions as well as the early righteous forebears never prohibited anything unless they were sure that it was categorically so. Otherwise, they used to recommend against it, or express their abhorrence of it, etc, but never categorically declared it *ḥarām.* Extremists, however, hastily prohibit without reservation, out of piety and coutiousness, if we take them to be well-meaning, or possibly out of other motives known only to Allah (SWT). If there are two opinions in Islamic jurisprudence about a certain issue, one declaring it *mubāḥ* and the other *makrūh,* the extremists abide by the latter; if it is declared *makrūḥ* by one and *ḥarām* by another, they also favor the latter. If there are two opinions, one which facilitates while the other makes things difficult, they also follow the latter. They persistently adhere to Ibn 'Umar's hard-line opinions, but never accept Ibn 'Abbās' facilitations. This tendency is largely due to their ignorance of the point of view which avails facilitation.

To illustrate this point, I would like to relate the following incident which I myself witnessed. One day, an extremist saw a man drinking water while he was standing. The extremist roughly asked him to sit down because such an action was a deviation from the Prophet's Sunnah. Confused, the man remained standing. He was then told that if he were a true Muslim, he would immediately induce vomiting to purify himself. At this point I gently intervened, telling the extremist: "The matter does not deserve this harshness. Standing is a minor controversial issue which does not deserve outright condemnation or harshness." The extremist then said that there is a *ḥadīth* which categorically forbid it, and require "whoever absentmindedly does so to induce vomiting."[17] My reply was: "But the *aḥādīth* which permit drinking while standing are more authentic and were therefore cited by al Bukhārī in a chapter in his *Ṣaḥīḥ* entitled "Drinking While Standing," but he cited none of the *aḥādīth* which forbade it. Furthermore, al Tirmidī as well as others, reported several *aḥādīth* which testify to this. It is also true that the Prophet (ṢA'AS) drank water while standing during his farewell *ḥajj.*[18] Moreover, it is narrated that 'Alī ibn Abū Ṭālib (RA'A) drank while standing and said "Some people dislike drinking while standing, but I saw the Prophet (ṢA'AS) doing it,

---

[17] Reported in the *Ṣaḥīḥ.*

[18] Reported by al Bukhārī and Muslim on the authority of Ibn 'Abbās.

just as you see me doing it now."[19]

Al Tirmidī also reported the permissibility of drinking while standing, basing this on the sayings and practices of a number of the companions of the Prophet (RA'A). According to al Tirmidī, Ibn 'Umar said: "During the time of the Prophet (ṢA'AS) we used to eat while walking and drink while standing."

Kabshah also said: "I came once upon the Prophet (ṢA'AS) and saw him drinking from a suspended waterskin."[20]

The interpretations handed down to us by the most reliable scholars of the ḥadīth show that although there is a clear encouragement to drink while sitting, there is no prohibition of drinking while standing. These scholars argue that the *aḥādīth* which encourage the former were revoked by other *aḥādīth,* and that this was confirmed by the practice by Abū Bakr, 'Umar, 'Uthmān and 'Alī (RA'A). Therefore, in such an entangled issue, it would be totally wrong to forbid a person to drink water while standing.

Similarly, many young people today engage in speculations about the proper Islamic dress. Such speculations are based on the following sound ḥadīth: "The part [of the garment which hangs] below the ankles is in the fire."[21] In their desire to adhere to this ḥadīth, many young people wear above-the-ankle garments and also seek to impose a similar style on people around them. Such pressure on others engenders ill-will on both sides, and charges of extremism or nonadherence to Islamic norms will certainly be leveled by both parties against each other. The *aḥādīth* which warn Muslims against wearing garments below the ankle, are qualified by other *aḥādīth* which, upon a deeper reading, reveal the reason for this prohibition. Below-the-ankle garments were once seen as manifestations of pride, arrogance, and extravagance.

For example, the Prophet (ṢA'AS) answered: "Allah will not look, on the Day of Resurrection, at the person who drags his garments [behind him] out of conceit."[22]

Abū Bakr (RA'A) once said to the Prophet (ṢA'AS): "My *izār* hangs low if I do not take care of it," and the Prophet (ṢA'AS) answered: "You are not of those who do so out of conceit."[23]

For this reason, al Nawawī and other Mulsim scholars contend that

---

[19] Reported by al Bukhārī and Muslim.

[20] Reported by al Tirmidhī.

[21] Reported by al Bukhārī on the authority of Abū Hurayrah.

[22] Reported by Muslim.

[23] Reported by al Bukhārī on the authority of 'Abd Allah ibn 'Umar.

wearing such a garment is *makrūh,* but a *makrūh* can become *mubāḥ* when there is a compelling reason.

3. Misconceptions

Such afore-mentioned examples of confused thinking and blurred vision of the fundamentals of Islam, its shari'ah and the aims of its message have led to many misconceptions in the minds of Muslim youth. Such misconceptions need to be fully explained and carefully defined as the form the basis of relating to others judging and reforming them. Some of the most important misconceptions include concepts like Islam, *īmān, kufr, nifāq,* and *jāhilīyah,* etc. Linguistic complexities or a lack of mastery of the Arabic language by some people have led to confusion and misunderstanding. The complexities of language escape the non-experts. Consequently, they become unable to differentiate between the figurative or metaphoric and the literal meanings, thereby confusing matters. They are unable to realize, for instance, the difference between absolute (or perfect) *īmān* and limited (or nominal) *īmān;* between perfect Islam and limited (or nominal) Islam between major *kufr* leading to non-Islam and the *kufr* of disobedience between major *shirk* and minor *shirk;* between hypocrisy of belief and hyprocrisy of action. They also equate the *jāhilīyah* of ethics and behavior with that of belief. The following is a brief clarification of these concepts[24] with a view to preventing dangerous consequences.

Absolute (or perfect) *īmān* combines what a person believes, says, and does. This is the kind of *īmān* referred to in the following Qur'ānic verses:

> For, believers are those who, when Allah is mentioned, feel a tremor in their hearts, and when they hear His signs rehearsed, find their faith strengthened and put [all] their trust in their Lord. (8:2).
>
> Successful indeed are the believers, those who humble themselves in their prayers (23:1-2).
>
> Only those are believers who have believed in Allah and His

---

[24] More detailed information can be found in my prospective book: *The Issue of Takfīr.*

Apostle, and have never since doubted, but have striven with their belongings and their persons in the cause of Allah: Such are the sincere ones (49:15).

The same concept of *īmān* is also expressed in the following *aḥādīth:*

> Anybody who believes in Allah and in the Last Day should keep good relations with kith and kin...he should say what is good or keep silent.[25]

In another, *īmān* is defined by negating what is not:

> None of you will have *īmān* until he wishes for his [Muslim] brother what he wishes for himself.[26]

The Prophet (ṢAʿAS) in another ḥadīth defines *īmān*:

> When an adulterer commits fornication, he does not have *īmān* at the time he is doing it; when somebody drinks alcoholic drink, he does not have *īmān* at the time of drinking; and when a thief steals, he does not have *īmān* at the time when he is stealing.[27]

It is important to notice that in the last two *ahādīth, īmān* is defined by negation. This means that the reference here is to absolute or perfect *īmān,* not to *īmān,* as when you say: "He who does not practically apply his knowledge is not a scholar." Negation here is of perfect knowledge rather than limited knowledge. Perfect *īmān* is also referred to in the following ḥadīth: *"Īmān* consists of seventy branches [i.e., parts] and *ḥayā*[28] is part of *īmān."* Abū Bakr al Bayhaqī in his book *al Jāmiʿ li Shuʿab al Īmān* likens *īmān* to a tree. The trunk symbolizes the fundamental articles of faith which represent religious observances, manners, ethics, and transactions. Just as a trunk is essential to the existence of the tree, so are the fundamental articles of faith essential to the believer. Conversely, since the tree could survive even in the absence of some of its branches, so a believer's status in the fold of Islam is in proportion to what remains of the branches of his *īmān.* The basic *īmān* was defined by Angel Jibrīl: *"Īmān* is to believe in Allah, his angels, books, messengers and the divine destiny."

---

[25] Reported by al Bukhārī on the authority of Abū Hurayrah.

[26] Reported by al Bukhārī on the authority of Anas Ibn Mālik.

[37] Reported by al Bukhārī on the authority of Abū Hurayrah.

[28] *Ḥayā'*: This term covers a large number of concepts which are to be taken together; among them are self-respect, modesty, bashfulness, scruples, etc.

Al Ḥāfiz ibn Ḥajar wrote in *Fatḥ al Bārī:*

> Our righteous forebears said: "*Īmān* is a belief in the heart, an utterance by tongue, and a practice of the fundamentals of faith." They meant that translation of *īmān* into practice is a requisite for its perfection. In this sense, they believed that *īmān* can increase or decrease. The Marjīyah contended that *īmān* is a belief and an utterance only; the Karamīyah believed that utterance is enough; the Mu'tazilah believed that it consists of practice, utterance, and belief. The difference between them and the righteous forebears is that the former considered practice as a necessary condition for the truthfulness of *īmān,* while the latter considered it as a necessary condition for its perfection. But perfection is only Allah's; for us, declaration of *īmān* in utterance is sufficient. Once this is done, the person is to be judged in accordance with the Shari'ah but cannot be considered a *kāfir* unless he commits an action of *kufr* , i.e., prostrates himself before an idol, which shows that he is still an unbeliever. If a person commits an act of sinfulness, short of apostasy or blasphemy, he may or may not be considered a believer depending on his utterance of *īmān;* a person may be judged as a non-believer according to the concept of perfect *īmān.* If a person is accused of *kufr* he is to be judged by comitting an action of *kufr.* If a person is exonerated from the accusation of *kufr,* he is to be judged according to his practice of *iman.*

Islam could signify a person's utterance of *shahādah* which is the gateway to Islam; a *kāfir* becomes a Muslim as soon as he witnesses that there is no god but Allah and that Muḥammad is His messenger, even before performing *ṣalāh* or giving *zakāh,* because these forms of *'ibādah* are only accepted from a Muslim. He only needs to accept these duties and commit himself to them, even if he does not practice them. It is the utterance of *shahādah* that secures protection of his life and property. The Prophet (ṢA'AS) said: "If they [people] utter it *[shahādah],* they safeguard their lives and properties from me so long as they fulfil its responsibilities. They are accountable to Allah."[29] The term, Islam, may also be used to mean the five pillars, as mentioned in the Prophet's noted hadith, narrated by Ibn 'Umar: "Islam is based on five pillars: to witness that there is no god but Allah and that Muḥammad is His

---

[29] Reported by al Bukhārī on the authority of Ibn 'Umar.

Messenger; to perform *ṣalāh;* to give *zakāh;* to do *ṣiyām* during Ramaḍān; and to perform *ḥajj.*"

Hadith literature contains Jibrīl's definition of Islam. When the Prophet (ṢAAS) asked Jibrīl to tell him about Islam, the latter said: "Islam is to worship Allah alone and to associate no other beings with Him, to perform *ṣalāh,* to give the ordained *zakāh,* and to do *ṣiyām* during Ramaḍān."[30] In Jibrīl's words we can find the difference between the concepts of *īmān* and Islam; it is also evident that the two terms can be used synonymously; if they are linked together each is implicit in the other. There is indeed no *īmān* without Islam, and no Islam without *īmān.*

Īmān pertains to the heart; Islam pertains to bodily action and outward behavior, as we can see from the following ḥadīth: "Islam is overt, *īmān* is [what is believed] in the heart."[31]

The same definition of *īmān* and Islam is found in the following Qur'ānic verse: "The desert Arabs say: 'We believe'. Say: 'You have no faith,' but you [only] say: 'We have submitted our wills to Allah, for not yet has faith entered your hearts" (49:14).

Islam can also be used to signify perfect Islam as in the following ḥadīth: "Islam is [the state when] your heart submits [completely] to Allah, and when you avoid harming Muslims with your tongue or hand." Also in two other *aḥadīth:* "A Muslim is the one who avoids harming Muslims with his tongue and hands," and: "You are a Muslim when you wish for people what you wish for yourself."

In juristic language, *kufr* signifies the rejection and denial of Allah (SWT) and His messages, as in the following Qur'ānic verses:

> Anyone who denies Allah, His angels, His books, His Apostles, and the Day of Judgment has gone far, far astray (4:136).

Kufr could also imply *riddah* (apostacy), and consequently the complete loss of *īmān:*

> If anyone rejects faith, fruitless is his work, and in the hereafter he will be in the ranks of those who have lost [all spiritual good]" (5:5).

Also:

> And if any of you turn back from their faith and die in unbelief, their works will bear no fruit in this life and in the hereafter. They will be companions of the fire and will abide therein (2:217).

---

[30] Reported by al Bukhārī on the authority of Abū Hurayrah.

[31] Reported by Aḥmad and al Bazzāz.

The term *kufr* is also used to denote transgressions which are short of a total rejection of Islam and do not amount to a rejection and denial of Allah (SWT) and His Messenger. The scholar Ibn al Qayyim divided *kufr* into two categories—major and minor.[32] Major *kufr* leads to eternal punishment in *Jahannam,* minor *kufr* leads to temporary rather than eternal punishement in *Jahannam.*

Consider the following *aḥādīth:* "Two things if practiced by my Ummah are manifestations of *kufr:* false accusation about a person's lineage and lamentation of the deed." And: "He who has anal sex with his wife commits *kufr* in what was revealed to Muḥammad." And: "If a person seeks a diviner or fortune-teller and believes in him or her, he commits *kufr* in what was revealed to Muḥammad."

And also: "Do not revert to *kufr* after my death by killing one another." This is the interpretation of Ibn 'Abbās as well as the majority of the Prophet's companions of the following Qur'ānic verse: "And if any fail to judge by [the light of] what Allah has revealed, they are [no better than] unbelievers" (5:44).

There are various interpretations of the above verse. Ibn 'Abbās says: "It is not *kufr* which excludes a person from the fold of Islam, but it has an element of *kufr* in it, because the person who commits it does not deny Allah and the Last Day." Ṭawūs exressed the same opinion. 'Atā' said: "This is *kufr* or an injustice or a *fisq* which can be greater or lesser in degree than another." Others, like 'Ikrimah, argued that those who do not judge in accordance with what Allah (SWT) has revealed commit *kufr.* But this argument is weak, because sheer rejection of Allah's revelation amounts to *kufr* whether a person has judged in the light of Sharī'ah or not. 'Abd al Azīz al Kinānī believes that *kufr* comprises negligence to judge in accordance with all that Allah (SWT) has revealed, including *tawḥīd* and Islam. But this is also farfetched, for the reference in the verse is to the rejection of all or part of what was revealed.

Al Baghawī reported that most jurists are agreed that the reference is to those who deliberately contradict the text of which they are neither ignorant nor confused. Qatādah and al Ḍaḥḥāk are of the opinion that *kufr* in the above verse refers to the People of the Book, i.e., the Jews and the Christians. But this contradicts even the literal meaning of the verse and therefore cannot be accepted. Some jurists maintain that it signifies a form of *kufr* which indeed excludes a person from the fold of Islam. Ibn al Qayyīm says:

---

[32] See his book *Madārij al Sālikīn.*

> Judging contrary to what Allah (SWT) has revealed contains both types of *kufr,* the major and the minor, according to the attitude of the person making the judgment. If he believes that a judgment must be passed according to what Allah (SWT) has revealed and a punishment decided, but refrains from doing so out of disobedience and transgression, in that case he commits minor *kufr.* But if he believes that it is not obligatory and that he is free to act, notwithstanding his conviction that it is divine, he then commits a major *kufr.* But if he acts out of ignorance, or makes an unintentional mistake, he is only to be judged as a wrongdoer.

The gist of the matter is that all transgressions and disobediance are types of *kufr* implying ingratitude, because gratitude requires compliance and obedience. Therefore, human endeavor could be manifest in gratitude, or in *kufr,* or in something other than the two. Only Allah (SWT) knows.

Shirk[33] is also divided into two categories: major and minor. Major *shirk* is basically to worship beings other than Allah (SWT) or to associate other beings with Him. It is the subject of the following Qur'ānic verse: "Allah does not forgive that partners should be set up with Him: but he forgives anything else to whom He pleases" (4:48). Minor *shirk* involves such practices as taking a sacred oath in the name of someone or something other than Allah (SWT), or believing in the power of amulets to bring good or bad fortune. This *shirk* is the subject of the following *aḥādīth:* "He who takes an oath in the name of any other than Allah commits *kufr,*"[34] and "He who wears an amulet commits *shirk,*"[35] and "Charms *(ruqā),* amulets *(tamā'im; ta'awiẓ),* and mascot *(tawlah)* are [all] *shirk.*"[36]

Nifāq (hypocrisy) is also major and minor. A major *nifāq* is to cherish *kufr* while pretending *īmān* in order to deceive: it is mentioned in the following Qur'ānic verses:

> Of the people, there are some who say: "We believe in Allah and the Last Day" but they do not [really] believe. Fain would they deceive Allah and those who believe, but they only deceive themselves and realize [it] not! (2:8-9).

and:

---

[33] *Shirk (Mushrik)*: "Association of other beings with Allah (SWT); opposite of *Tawḥīd*.

[34] Reported by Abū Dāwūd, al Tirmidhī, and al Ḥākim.

[35] Reported by Aḥmad, and al Ḥākim.

[36] Reported by Ibn Ḥabbān and al Ḥākim who asserts that its *isnād* is authentic.

When they meet those who believe, they say: "We believe"; but when they are alone with their evil ones, they say: "We are really with you. We [were] only jesting" (2:14).

This is the kind of *nifāq* which is mentioned in *Sūrat al Munāfiqīn,* as well as in other Qur'ānic verses. It is the same *nifāq* which Allah (SWT) promises to punish:

The hypocrites will be in the lowest depths of the Fire: You will find no helper for them (4:145).

Minor *nifāq* signifies the *nifāq* of believers, i.e. the behavior of a Muslim who genuinely believes in Allah (SWT) and in the hereafter, but retains hypocritical characteristics. This is best described in the following *aḥādīth:*

The signs of a *munāfiq* are three: whenever he speaks, he tells lies; whenever he promises, he breaks his promise; and if he is trusted, he proves to be dishonest.[37]

Whoever has the following four characteristics will be a blatant *munāfiq,* and whoever has one of these characteristics will have an element of *nifāq,* until he gives it up: if he speaks, he tells a lie; if he is trusted, he betrays; if he makes a convenant, he proves treacherous; and if he disagrees, he behaves in a very impudent, evil, and insulting manner.[38]

This is the kind of *nifāq* which the companions of the Prophet (ṢA'AS) and our righteous forbears feared most. They said in describing it: "None but a *munāfiq* will rest assured against this kind of *nifāq* which is only feared by a true believer.

4. Emphasis on Allegorical Texts

It is important to point out here that a root cause of extremism and of misunderstanding of religious matters, in the past as well as in the present, is emphasis on allegorial texts and disregard of the categorical ones: the allegorial ones are those with implicated and unclear meanings; the categorical are those whose meanings are clear, manifest and defined. Laying emphasis on allegorical texts cannot be the attitude of

[37] Agreed upon and reported on the authority of Abū Hurayrah.

[38] Agreed upon and reported on the authority of 'Abd Allah ibn 'Umar.

those with knowledge and insight, but of those who cherish deviation in their hearts. The Qur'ān states:

> He it is Who has sent down to you [Muḥammad] the Book: in it are verses basic or fundamental [of established meaning]; they are the foundation of the Book; others are allegorical. But those in whose hearts is perversity follow the part thereof that is allegorical, seeking discord, and searching for hidden meanings, but no one knows its true meanings except Allah (3:7).

Extremists and innovators of old used such allegorical texts as their final evidence, neglecting and overlooking the fundamental categorical ones. Extremists today do exactly the same: using the allegorical to define and determine important concepts which result in serious and grave consequences when used as bases for judging individuals or groups, for assessing their behavior, and for classifying them as either friends or enemies, believers or *kuffār* who must be fought.

Such shallowness in understanding and hastiness in making judgments, without careful investigation or comparision (since the fundamental, categorical texts were neglected, and only the allegorical considered) caused the Khawarij to fall into the trap of *takfīr,* considering all Muslims but themselves as *kuffār.* On the basis of strange "religious" notions and delusions, they fought the great Muslim 'Alī ibn Abū Ṭālib (RA'A), although they were among his followers and soldiers. The main reason for their disagreement with 'Alī (RA'A) was his decision to accept arbitration to settle his differences with Mu'āwiyah ibn Abū Sufyān in order to maintain the unity of his army and to save the lives of Muslims on both sides. The Khawārij, however, rejected any arbitration because of their misunderstanding and misinterpretation of the Qur'ānic verse: "...the command is for none but Allah" (12:40), and accused 'Alī (RA'A), one of the first Muslims to give in the cause of Islam his essential support, of deviation. 'Alī replied to their citing of the above verse with his famous saying: "A word of truth twisted to serve *bāṭil* [falsehood]."

The fact that the command and all authority in all matters are for Allah (SWT) alone does not mean that human beings are forbidden from arbitrating and judging subsidiary issues within the framework and injunctions of the Sharī'ah. 'Abd Allah ibn 'Abbās, who had deep insight into and knowledge of Sharī'ah, debated the Khawārij on this issue and refuted their arguments, citing and referring to verses in the Qur'ān which sanction various types of arbitration.

The following verse, for instance, sanctions arbitration to settle differences between a husband and a wife:

> If you fear a breach between them twain, appoint [two] arbiters, one from his family and the other from hers. If they wish for peace, Allah will cause their reconciliation (4:35).

Another instance of arbitration can be seen in the discretion that the arbitrators can exercise in judging a pilgrim who hunts and kills while in pilgrim garb:

> O you who believe! Kill not game while in the sacred precincts or in pilgrim garb. If any of you does so intentionally, the compensation is an offering, brought to the Ka'bah, of a domestic animal equivalent to the one he killed, as adjudged by two just men among you; or by way of atonement, the feeding of the indigent, or its equivalent in fasts, that he may taste of the penalty of his deed (5:95).

Some people who do not carefully examine and contemplate the Qur'ān and *Sunnah* and consider them in their entirety, seeking balance between the affirmed and the negated, comparing the specific with the general or the absolute with the limited, believing well meaningfully in the categorical and the allegorical; All such careless people will inevitably go astray, lose clarity of vision, and make haphazard judgements.

This is the trap into which those who nowadays hasten to brand others with *kufr* have fallen, and into which the Khawārij of old fell. According to al Shāṭibī, the fundamental cause behind this extremism is ignorance of, and undue presumptions about, the purposes and meanings of Sharī'ah, which cannot be the practice of a person who is versed in Islamic knowledge.

It is worthwhile to reiterate the case of the Khawārij to whom reference has already been made. Is it indeed instructive to contemplate how they "slipped out of religion as an arrow would slip out of its kill," which testifies to the Prophet's description of them as those "who recite the Qur'ān but [its teachings] never touch their hearts." This probably means – and Allah (SWT) knows best – that their verbal recitation of the Qur'ān is just a physical exercise that never influences or affects them. This also recalls the previously quoted ḥadīth about, "...taking away of knowledge."

This interpretation is in tune with one advanced by Ibn 'Abbās (RA'A) as reported by Ibrahīm al Taymī both in Abū 'Ubayd's *Faḍā'il al Qur'ān,* and in Sa'īd ibn Manṣūr's interpretation of the Qur'an:

> 'Umar ibn al Khaṭṭāb once wondered, while sitting alone, why people who follow one Prophet and turn their faces to the same *qiblah* in *ṣalāh* are tormented with disagreement. 'Umar then sent to Ibn 'Abbās and asked him: "Why should this Ummah be tormented by disagreement when it has the same Prophet and the same *qiblah?"* (Sa'īd adds to this "and the same Book.") Ibn 'Abbās answered: "The Qur'ān was revealed and we read it and comprehended the reasons for its revelation. But there will come people who will read the Qur'ān and fail to understand the occasions and subjects of revelation. As a result they will make different interpretations and will, therefore, disagree.

Sa'īd ibn Mansūr added:

> Ibn 'Abbās said; "Every group of people will have an opinion about the Qur'an , which will lead to disagreement, and then to fighting." But 'Umar and 'Alī, who were also present, did not like this [Ibn 'Abbās'] ominous explanation and they reproached him. But no sooner had Ibn 'Abbās left than it occurred to 'Umar that there might be some truth in what he said. He sent for him again and asked him to reiterate what he had told them earlier. After careful consideration, 'Umar recognized and appreciated what Ibn 'Abbās said.

Al Shāṭibī wrote:

> Ibn 'Abbās was right. When a person knows the reason behind a certain verse or *sūrah,* he knows how to interpret it and what its objectives are. However, ignorance of that leads people to misinterpret it and to have different opinions, without an insight and knowledge which could lead them to the truth and prevent them from indulging ignorantly in such matters with no support or evidence,and therefore go astray and lead people astray.
>
> This can be demonstrated by what is reported by Ibn Wahab from Bakīr who asked Nāfi': "What does Ibn 'Umar think of the Ḥarūrīyah, i.e., the Khawārij, who were also called the Ḥarūrīyah after the place—*Ḥarūrā'*—where they gathered and were fought by 'Alī ibn Abū Ṭālib and the companions of the Prophet (ṢAAS) who supported him?" Nāfi' answered:

"He [ibn 'Umar] thinks they are the most evil of people. They applied the verses which pertain to the *kuffār* to the believers." Sa'īd ibn Jubayr explained this, saying that among the allegorical verses misinterpreted by the Khawārij are: "If any do fail to judge [by the light of] what Allah has revealed, they are [no better than] wrongdoers" (5:44), which they usually combine with "Yet those who reject Faith hold [others] as equal with their Guardian-Lord" (6:1). Therefore they reached the conclusion that if a ruler does not rule justly he commits *kufr,* and he who commits *kufr* associates others with Allah and therefore commits *shirk.* On this basis they declare people *mushrikūn* and fight and kill them. This indeed is the kind of misinterpretation and misunderstanding which Ibn 'Abbās has warned against, and which results from ignorance of the meaning intended in the revelation.

Nāfi' said: "Whenever Ibn 'Umar was asked about the Ḥārurīyyah, he used to say: 'They declare Muslims as *kuffār,* sanction the shedding of their blood and the confiscation of their property; they marry women during their *'iddah;*[39] and marry women who are already married and whose husbands are still alive. I know of no other people who deserve to be fought more than them."[40]

5. The Need To Acknowledge and Respect Specialization

One of the causes of the extremists' shallowness and lack of insight is that they never listen to people who hold different views, never accept any dialogue with them, and never imagine that their own views could be tested in the light of others and be either contradicted or refuted. Many of them have not been taught by reliable Muslim *'ulamā'* specialized in the field. Rather, they have received semi-knowledge directly from books and newspapers without any opportunity for revision or discussion which could test the learner's understanding and analyze the depth

[39] *'Iddah*: "Legally prescribed period of waiting during which a woman may not marry after being widowed or divorced."

[40] See Abū Isḥaq al Shāṭibī, *al I'tiṣām*, 2:182-184.

of his knowledge. They simply read, "understand," and then deduce what they wish. However their reading, understanding, and deduction may well be wrong or deficient.

There might be someone somewhere who opposes their opinions on stronger and more valid foundations, but they are not aware of that because nobody has drawn their attention to such a possibility. These devout young people have ignored the fact that if they want to study Sharī'ah, they must seek the help of reliable Muslim scholars. They cannot venture into this extensive and sophisticated discipline without the guidance of such reliable scholars who can interpret and explain obscurities, define terms, and point out similarities and the relationships between the parts and the whole. Those who venture into it alone will meet with the same catastrophic results which would certainly befall the unskilled swimmer who ventures into deep waters. Proper knowledge of Sharī'ah cannot be perfected without practice and close contact with the experts, especially in those areas where opinions diverge, evidences seem to contradict each other, and certain matters seem to be confusing. This is why our forebears *'ulamā'* have warned us not to seek to study and understand the Qur'ān through a person who has only memorized it without any knowledge of its contents, nor to seek knowledge through a person who has acquired his own "knowledge" from reading books and journals only, without being properly tutored by reputable and qualified scholars.

Seeking knowledge of Islam alone and only through books reflects the young people's complete loss of confidence in the professional *'ulamā'* and learned scholars, especially those patronized by the authorities, because they believe that such people have lost the courage to disagree with rulers who go astray. Not only are the religious scholars silent about rulers' atrocities and their negligence of Sharī'ah, but they too often—and quite hypocritically—glorify and commend them for such deplorable actions. It would be better for such *'ulamā'* to at least keep silent rather than to support *bāṭil* (falsehood).

It is not surprising therefore, that young Muslims have decided that they can only trust past rather than present-day *'ulamā',* and consequently have sought the former's books for knowledge and guidance. When I once asked one of these devout young Muslims why they do not try to seek knowledge through learned *'ulamā',* he said to me: "And where do we find the *'ulamā'* we can trust? There are only those who are puppets in the hands of rulers; those who unscrupulously give *fatāwā* to permit or to prohibit in accordance with the whims and wishes of rulers; those who bless socialism and consider it Islamic should the ruler happen to be a socialist, but should he happen to be a capitalist then capitalism is blessed and considered Islamic! Those *'ulamā'* who declare that peace with the enemy is *ḥarām* and *munkar* when a ruler decides to wage war, but quickly give support and blessings for such peace when the ruler's policy is changed; those who '...make it lawful one year, and forbidden another year...' (9:37); those *'ulamā'* who have equated between the mosque and the church, between Muslim Pakistan and pagan India!"

My reply to this was: "We should not generalize. There are indeed *'ulamā'* who have condemned *bāṭil,* stood up against oppression, and refused to compromise with or support dictators, in spite of all intimidations and temptations. Many of these *'ulamā'* were imprisoned, subjected to all sorts of torture, and even fell martyrs for the cause of Islam." The young man—though admitting that that is true—insisted that the power to guide, advise, and give *fatāwā* is still in the hands of the former instead of the latter, i.e., the deviant so-called "eminent" *'ulamā'.*

One however cannot but admit that there is a great deal of truth in what the young man claimed. Most of the "eminent" *'ulamā'* who are entrusted with leadership and guidance have become mere pawns in the hands of those in authority, who direct them as they wish. Such *'ulamā'* need to know that keeping silent about the truth is synonymous with uttering *bāṭil;* both are Satanic evils. In a debate on Egyptian television on "family planning" and "birth control" from the point of view of Sharī'ah, one of the speakers, a well-known Muslim scholar, asked—to the astonishment of the chairman—whether the aim of the debate was to advocate or oppose "family planning," so that he could be on his guard! May Allah (SWT) bless the preceding generation of *'ulamā',* one of whom courageously addressed a very influential member of the regime in Egypt in the past saying: "He who stretches his legs to look for work does not need to stretch his hands to beg." One wishes that the contemporary scholars who have been deficient in belief and piety could enrich and deepen their knowledge, in general, and *fiqh* in particular!

The fact is that devout young people who genuinely desire to deepen their knowledge of Islam have come in contact with well-known *'ulamā',* illustrious in the circles of rhetoric and letters, only to find that the latter's knowledge of the Qur'ān and Sunnah is seriously deficient.

One of those *'ulamā'* wrote in a daily newspaper claiming that there is no usury in transactions between a government and its subjects. He presumptuously deduced that since there is no usury between father and son, one could say that there is no usury between a government and its subjects. But the context of father and son, which this man based his argument on, is controversial and has been the subject of considerable disagreement. It is not supported by an authentic text or by consensus. How then could it be taken as a foundation upon which other matters could be analyzed and judged by analogy? Even if it could be taken as a criterion, it should have been differential analogy.

In view of this, one has to admit that the youths' disappointment in and despair of such people who are devoid of both piety and knowledge are justified. They have found that some of these *'ulamā'* would cite *aḥādīth* spurious in content or *isnād* and disregard the authentic ones which are agreed upon by all. Some would seek cheap popularity by appealing to the desires of the masses and the "elite" and never seek knowledge from its proper source. For these reasons, the young have lost confidence in them and in everything they say. Even some reputable *'ulamā'* whom the young used to respect and admire fell into the trap and were lured by the media to voice and express their support for the authorities, throwing all the blame on the young without listening to their arguments or points of view, or even trying to understand the reasons behind their attitudes.

On another occasion, after the Egyptian government had imprisoned many members of various Islamic groups and suspended their activities, one of the well-known *'ulamā'* declared in a public meeting that the Islamic groups were forsaken by Allah (SWT). He argued that if they were following the right path and were blessed by Allah (SWT), neither the police nor the army could have defeated them. Such an absurdity is no criterion for judging between truth and *bāṭil,* and is downright un-Islamic.

There are many conditions and means which could lead to victory, but these may not be available to the person or group fighting for the truth, and thus they may encounter defeat. Alternatively, a person or group fighting for falsehood may be helped to triumph by certain circumstances; but such a victory can never last, however long it may endure. The ups and downs of current history amply demonstrate this. In these days defeat and victory are not determined by truth and falsehood; they are determined by the interference of superpowers. Indeed, the "victories" of Israel over the Arabs are a case in point.

Do we not all know how the committed Muslim Turks and their *'ulamā'* were mercilessly crushed by Ataturk and his gang? And how Islam was elbowed out of the homeland of the caliphate to be forcefully replaced by irreligious secularism that was insidiously perpetrated upon the Turkish people? Which of the two sides was following the truth, and which was following *bāṭil*? Recently, some venerable *'ulamā'* were tortured and sentenced to death in a Muslim country because they opposed a "family law" which the government intended to enforce even though it was a stark deviation from Sharī'ah. The punishment was intended to terrorize and silence all who opposed this law. The despotic authority achieved its objective and other *'ulamā',* indeed all the people, were silenced. Does this mean that the government was right and the sentenced *'ulamā'* wrong? In another Muslim country, the non-Muslim minority rules the Muslim majority. Thousands of Muslim men as well as women are arrested and terrorized daily to suppress any opposition or rejection. When prisons are full, these men and women are liquidated. Moreover, to humiliate and coerce such devout Muslims as those who do not fear death and even torture, the authorities resort to heinous atrocities the likes of which were not committed even by murderers like Hülagü, Genghiz Khān, or others; they rape their daughters, sisters, or wives in front of them.

O God! How many innocent people were killed? How many sacrosanctities were dishonored? How many sacred precincts were debased? How many time-honored mosques were demolished? How much precious wealth robbed? How many homes – indeed whole cities – were wrecked on their inhabitants? How many men, women, and innocent children were subjected to atrocities? This is the course of history, indeed of Islamic history.

Al Ḥusayn ibn 'Alī (RA'A) was defeated by the army led by Ibn Ziyād, one of the commanders of Yazīd ibn Abū Sufyān. As a result, Banū Umayyah ruled for decades, but the descendants of the Prophet (ṢA'AS) were not given any reprieve even during the reign of the 'Abbāsīyīn, their cousins. Could this be cited as evidence that Yazīd was following the truth while al Ḥusayn (RA'A) was following *bāṭil*?

Furthermore, years later the courageous and learned commander 'Abd Allah ibn al Zubayr was defeated by the unscrupulous al Ḥajjāj ibn Yūsuf. Then al Ḥajjāj crushed another great Muslim commander, 'Abd al Raḥmān ibn al Ash'ath, as well as a group of prominent *'ulamā'* which included Sa'īd ibn Jubayr, al Sha'bī, Muṭrif ibn 'Abd Allah, and many others. All of these defeats were great losses to the Ummah, especially Sa'īd ibn Jubayr of whom al Imām Aḥmad said: "Sa'īd was killed at a time when every Muslim was in great need of his knowledge and learning."

It is pertinent to mention here what some Muslims said when they were overpowered by their enemies during a battle: "By Allah! Even if we were torn into pieces by wolves we would never doubt the truth of our convictions and the falsity of your claims." When Ibn al Zubayr and a few of his followers were besieged in Makkah, he said: "By Allah, the righteous will never be degraded even if the whole world collaborated against them. And by Allah, the wrongdoers will never be rightly honored even if the moon appeared on their foreheads!"

This is in keeping with what the Qur'ān tells us of the fates of various prophets who were killed by their own people:

> Is it that whenever there comes to you a messenger with what yourselves desire not, you are puffed up with pride? Some you called imposters, and others you slay! (2:87).

Among such prophets were Zakarīyā ('AS) and his son Yaḥyā ('AS). Could it be said that the killing of these prophets and the success of their enemies indicate that the formers' stand was false? We also read in the Qur'ān the story of *Aṣḥāb al 'Ukhdūd* ('the Makers of the Pit') who made pits of fire and threw the believers alive into them while they sat around sadistically enjoying the bizarre spectacle: "And they ill-treated them for no other reason than that they believed in Allah, exalted in power, worthy of all praise!" (85:8).

Were these tyrants right because they defeated helpless believers and eliminated them? Were the believers wrong because their end was so bizarre? There are instances in the Qur'ān which show that the believers are sometimes tested by mishaps, and that the unbelievers are tempted by success.

Allah (SWT) says:

> Do men think that they will be left alone on saying: "We believe," and that they will not be tested? We did test those before them, and Allah will certainly know those who are true from those who are false (29:2-3).

After the defeat of the Muslims in the battle of Uḥud, the following verse was revealed:

> If a wound has touched you, be sure a similar wound has touched the others. Such days [of varying fortunes] we give to men and men by turns: that Allah may know those that believe, and that He may take to Himself from your ranks martyr-witnesses [to truth]. . . (3:140).

Allah (SWT) also says of the unbelievers:

> . . .by degrees shall We punish them from directions they perceive not (68:44).

6. Lack of Insight into History, Reality and the *Sunan* of Allah

In addition to the lack of insight into the true teachings of Islam, we could add the lack of insight into reality, life, and history as well as into Allah's *sunan* in His creation. In the absence of such insight, some people will continue to seek or demand the impossible and unavailable. They will imagine what does not or cannot happen, misunderstand occurrences and events, and interpret them on the basis of certain latent illusions which are not related in any way to Allah's *sunan* or to the essence of Sharī'ah. They want to change the whole fabric of society: its thought, traditions, ethics, systems; they also want to change its social, political, and economic systems by illusory means and imaginary methods. To realize these unrealistic objectives they show the courage, daring, and sacrifice to brave death and disregard any consequences for or against them, so long as their intentions and goals are for Allah's sake and for His message. Hence, it is not surprising that such people venture into actions which others refer to as either "suicidal" or "crazy", in total disregard of the numbers that fall victims thereof.

If such Muslims would but contemplate for a moment and heed the Sunnah of the Prophet (ṢA'AS), they would surely find their guidance. We need to be reminded that the Prophet (ṢA'AS) spent thirteen years in Makkah instructing and calling people to the message and even performing *ṣalāh* and *ṭawāf* at the Ka'bah, although it was surrounded at the time by more than 360 idols. Aware of the insignificance of his physical power as compared to that of his enemies, he never decided on a commando attack to destroy the idols. He was perceptive enough to realize that to do so was to endanger himself as well as his followers. Moreover, the physical destruction of the idols—which could easily be replaced—would not blot out the polytheism which was ingrained in the minds and hearts of his fellow tribesmen. He therefore endeavored to liberate their minds and thought from the fetters of superstition and paganism. Thus the Prophet (ṢA'AS) ignored the idols and concentrated his efforts on teaching monotheism and on purifying the pagan heart through piety, so that those who embraced the message would constitute a nucleus of believers who knew what they were fighting for; a group sure of success through patience and perseverance; a group that would neither be intoxicated by victory nor despondent over defeat. Indeed, there was a time when his companions, outraged by the brutalities which the pagans had inflicted upon them, requested his permission to fight back, but he always refused, realizing that the time was not yet ripe and that they had to endure until Allah (SWT) gave the permission for fighting.

One day, the Prophet (ṢA'AS) came upon 'Ammār ibn Yāsir (RA'A) and his parents being tortured by the unbelievers. All that he did at the time was to encourage them to endure patiently, and to give them good tidings about their assured place in *Jannah*. Things continued in this manner until the Muslims were permitted to fight in defense of their freedom and religion:

> To those against whom war is made, permission is given [to fight], because they are wronged—and verily, Allah is powerful for their aid—[They are] those who have been expelled from their homes in defiance of right, [for no cause] except that they say, "Our Lord is Allah" (22:39-40).

But this permission was only given after the Prophet (ṢA'AS) and his companions had managed to establish a home for themselves and increase their power and authority. Thereupon they were allowed to fight their enemies. They gained one victory after another until Allah (SWT) granted them *fatḥ*[41] of Makkah (from which the Prophet (ṢA'AS) had emigrated under the pressure of persecution), destroying the idols therein and reciting the following Qur'ānic verse:

> And say: "Truth has [now] come, and falsehood perished: for falsehood is [by its nature] bound to perish" (17:81).

This is the pattern of history which *Jamā'at al Takfīr wa al Hijrah* group in Egypt (since the late 1960's), strangely enough, considers unworthy to accept or emulate. Such a strange and absurd attitude is the cause of the difference between two of the leading men of the group, 'Abd al Raḥmān Abū al Khayr and Shaykh Shukrī, its founder. In his "Reminiscence," Abū al Khayr records that the group's "lack of confidence in and reliance on Islamic history" was the fourth aspect of the difference between him and Shaykh Shukrī, who considered Islamic history "a series of unauthentic events." History, for Shukrī, consists only of the stories narrated in the Qur'ān, and therefore he prohibited any interest in or

---

[41] *Fatḥ*: The act of granting (as in *Fataḥa*) or the victory or breakthrough granted. *Al Futūḥāt* (pl.): The moral and material victories granted to the Prophet Muḥammad (ṢA'AS) and his early followers, and hence the embracing of Islam of large masses of the population of any country or religion.

study of the periods of the Islamic caliphate[42].

Reflect on such an unreasonable, narrow-minded, and shallow conception, one which considers—on "religious grounds"—the study of Islamic history *ḥarām*. A history of a nation, with all its positive and negative aspects, its victories and defeats, is a rich mine upon which that nation draws in order to reconstruct and redirect its present. A nation which neglects its history is like a person who has lost his memory; or like a nation without roots or sense of belonging or direction. How could any group make such an unhealthy and abnormal condition the basis of its survival? Further, history is the mirror in which Allah's *sunan* are reflected in the whole universe in general and in human life in particular. This is why the Qur'ān has given special attention to the impact of the historical perspective and the wisdom that can be drawn from it. There are various Qur'ānic references to this. Let us contemplate the following verses:

> Many were the ways of life that have passed away before you: travel through the earth, and see what was the end of those who rejected Truth (3:137).

Allah's *sunan*, however, are characterized by consistency—they never change or alter:

> They swore their strongest oaths by Allah that if a warner came to them, they would follow his guidance better than any [other] of the peoples: but when a warner came to them, it only increased their flight [from righteousness], on account of their arrogance in the land and their plotting of evil. But the plotting of evil will hem in only the authors thereof. Now are they but looking for the way the ancients were dealt with? But no change will you find in Allah's way [of dealing]; no turning off will you find in Allah's way [of dealing] (35:42-43).

As Allah's *sunan* are common factors for all, His ways of dealing with those who follow evil are the same in all cases and apply to all people irrespective of their religion, as well as of time and space. We have an instructive example in the battle of Uḥud, when the Muslims paid dearly for disregarding the Prophet's advice, and which is clearly pointed out in the Qur'ān:

> What! When a single disaster smites you, although you smote

---

[42] See page 35 of Abū al Khayr's reminiscence about "*Jamā'at al Muslimīn*" the name by which the group is called by its advocates and followers.

[your enemies] with one twice as great, do you say: "Whence is this?" Say [to them]: "It is from yourselves: for Allah has power over all things" (3:165).

Another verse makes clear the nature of the mistake which led to their defeat:

> Allah did indeed fulfil His promise to you when you with His permission were about to annihilate your enemy,–until you flinched and fell to disputing about the order and disobeyed it... (3:152).

The assertion that history is a series of doubtful events may be true with respect to some trivial incidents, but the general direction and the fundamental events are well known and are well authenticated by more than one source. Even those events which are doubtful can be investigated by the learned in order to determine the truth and to sift out any errors, fabrications, or exaggerations.

However, we are not only concerned with Islamic history but with the whole history of humanity, that of Muslims and non-Muslims, ever since the beginning of creation. Wisdom is not drawn from the history of the believers alone, but from that of the atheists as well as from both the pious and the profligate, because Allah's *sunan*–like natural patterns–operate upon both parties without any favoritism towards the monotheist or the pagan.

Indeed, we cannot comprehend the Qur'ān properly or acknowledge with gratitude the favor conferred upon us by Islam unless we understand the erroneous nature and practices of *jāhilīyah*[43] referred to in the following verses:

> ...While, before that, they had been in manifest error (3:164).

And:

> ...And you were on the brink of a pit of fire, and He saved you from it (3:103).

This is also the essence of the following saying by 'Umar ibn al Khaṭṭāb (RA'A): "The bonds of Islam will be undone, one by one, as some Muslims become ignorant with [the evil nature of] *jāhilīyah* [and fail to appreciate Islam]."

Although many of the people concerned about Islam and its propaga-

---

[43] *Al Jāhilīyah*: "The order or regime in which the law of Allah (SWT) is not in force; pre-Islamic Arabia."

tion have neither carefully studied nor comprehended history, they nevertheless have not prohibited its study by themselves or by their followers as some extremists have done. The study of history is not just a recognition of events in their time sequence, but an activity that requires insight and perception into the events in order to comprehend their essence, draw wisdom from them, and spell out Allah's *sunan* in them. Mere observation of the ruins of earlier nations serves no purpose. The following verse shows that insight into history cannot be realized by such observations or by simply hearing about them:

> Do they not travel through the land, so that their hearts [and minds] may thus learn wisdom and their ears may thus learn to hear? Truly it is not their eyes that are blind, but their hearts which are in their breasts (22:46).

Historical occurrences repeat themselves and resemble each other because they are governed by consistent laws which set them in motion and adjust them. This is why Westerners say: "History repeats itself," and the Arabs express the same notion: "Tonight is similar to last night."

The Qur'ān refers to the observable similarity in attitudes, utterances, and actions due to the similarity of the thoughts and visions which emanate from them:

> Those without knowledge say: "Why does not Allah speak unto us? Or, why does not a sign come unto us?" So said the people before them words of similar import. Their hearts are alike. We have indeed made the signs clear unto any people who hold firmly to faith [in their hearts] (2:118).

Allah (SWT) also said of the pagans of Quraysh:

> Similarly, no messenger came to the peoples before them, but they said [of him] in like manner: "A sorcerer or one possessed!" Is this the legacy they transmitted to one another? Nay, they are themselves a people transgressing beyond bounds (51:52-53).

This similarity between the attitudes of the former and the latter nations toward Allah's messengers and the hastiness with which the people accused the messengers of sorcery or madness is not the result of transmitted legacy between the two, but because both are unjust and transgressing. Since the cause, i.e., transgression, is common to both, the attitude is the same.

Those who comprehend the importance of history and the operation of Allah's *sunan* in it can—and should—learn from the mistakes of past generations. Happy will be those who take a lesson and a warning from the mistakes and misfortunes of others and seek, nevertheless, to adopt their good. Wisdom, wherever he finds it, is a believer's goal, because he is more worthy of it than anyone else.

7. Two Important *Sunan*

Hasty enthusiastic Muslims usually overlook two important *sunan*, i.e. gradation and that achieving goals requires the allowance of due time. First: Gradation is clearly manifest in the process of creation as well as in legislation. Allah (SWT) is able to create the heavens and the earth in less than the twinkling of an eye: "Be, and it is" (2:117). Yet He created them in six of His days, i.e., in stages, known only to Him because they are different from our concept of "day." Gradation is also apparent in the creation of all living organisms which grow in stages until they reach maturity. The same process can also be seen in *da'wah*, which began with the inculcation of monotheism to liberate the minds from the fetters of paganism and superstition. When that was firmly established, *wājibāt* and *muḥarramāt* were then gradually introduced, as in the case of *ṣalāh, ṣiyām, zakāh*, and the prohibition of alcohol, etc. And in this we see the difference between Makkī and Madanī[44] texts.

'Ā'ishah (RA'A), describes the process of gradation in the introduction of Sharī'ah and the revelation of the Qur'ān: "The first Qur'ānic verses to be revealed were those in which *Jannah* and *Jahannam* were mentioned. [Later], when people embraced Islam, verses dealing with *ḥalāl* and *ḥarām* were revealed. If verses prohibiting drinking alcohol and practicing fornication were revealed first, people would have said, 'We would never give up drinking or fornication.'"[45]

Hence those who call for the return to the Islamic way of life and the establishment of the Islamic state must take into consideration the necessity of gradation for the realization of their goals, taking into account the sublimity of the goal, their own means and potential, and the multiplicity of impediments. This brings to mind the example set by the righteous Caliph, 'Umar ibn 'Abd al 'Azīz, who successfully reconstructed

---

[44] *Al Makkī* and *al Madanī*: "Said of the verses revealed in Makkah or in Madīnah, respectively."

[45] Reported by al Bukhārī.

life on the model set up by the *Rightly-Guided* Caliphs. But the process of reconstruction was not easy. Even his own son, 'Abd al Mālik, a very devout and enthusiastic Muslim, thought that his father was too slack in his attempts to eradicate all traces of deviation and aggression. He once addressed his father saying: "O, father, why don't you implement [reforms swiftly]? By Allah, I would not care if you and I perish for the sake of the truth." But 'Umar replied: "Do not be hasty my son. Allah condemned alcohol twice in the Qur'ān and prohibited it only on the third time. I fear if I force all the truth on people [at once] they would reject it all at once. This may cause *fitnah*."[46]

Second: The second of these *sunan* is complementary to the first, i.e., everything has an appointed term during which it reaches ripeness and maturity. This applies to the material as well as the moral. Nothing should be harvested before its appointed time; crops cannot be harvested before they have ripened. Rather than being useful, unripe fruit and vegetables can cause harm. And just as crops need time – sometimes a long time – to mature, the true meanings and values of great actions become apparent only after many years. The longer actions take to mature, the greater they are. The endeavors of one generation often materialize in the following one, or even much later. There is indeed no harm in this if everything takes its planned natural course. During the Prophet's early days in Makkah, the unbelievers used to mock him whenever he warned them of the punishment awaiting them if they persisted in rejecting Allah (SWT), and therefore they asked him to hasten this punishment, not realizing that it must take its course and could neither be delayed nor hastened:

> They ask you to hasten on the punishment [for them]: had it not been for a term [of respite] appointed, the punishment would certainly have come to them: and it will certainly reach them, of a sudden, while they perceive not! (29:53).

And:

> Yet they ask you to hasten on the punishment! But Allah will not fail in His promise. Verily, a day in the sight of your Lord is like a thousand years of your reckoning (22:47).

At this stage Allah (SWT) advised the Prophet (ṢA'AS) to persevere just as the earlier prophets had done and not to hasten in invoking Allah's punishment on them:

> Therefore patiently persevere, as did [all] the messengers of

[46] Al Shāṭibi's *Al Muwāfaqāt* 2:94.

> inflexible purpose; and be in no haste about the [unbelievers] (46:35).

Allah (SWT) reminded the Prophet (ṢA'AS) and his followers of the unflinching perserverance of earlier prophets in the face of hardships, the prolonged struggle, and the difficulty of awaiting victory:

> Or do you think you shall enter the garden [of bliss] without such [trials] as came to these before you? They encountered suffering and adversity and were so shaken in spirit that even the Messenger and those of faith who were with him cried, "When will the help of Allah come?" Verily, the help of Allah is [always] near (2:214).

Indeed, Allah's ordained victory is near, but it has an appointed time known only to Him, for He does not hasten things as His creatures do. For this reason, the Prophet (ṢA'AS) used to advise his companions to be patient and not to expect victory before its appointed time. The following incident demonstrates this point: When Khabāb ibn al Arat complained to the Prophet (ṢA'AS) of the great suffering which he encountered for the sake of Islam and asked him to invoke Allah (SWT) for help, the Prophet (ṢA'AS) was so angry that his face became red and he said:

> [A believer] before you used to be cut off with iron cutting tools so that nothing of his flesh or nerves remained beyond his bones, and another used to be sawed (alive) into two parts, but neither would abandon his religion. By Allah, He will surely make Islam prevail so that a traveler from Ṣan'ā [in the Yemen] to Ḥaḍramawt [in Oman] will not fear [during his journey] anything except Allah, and the wolf for his sheep. But you are [always] impatient.[47]

8. Islam: A Stranger in Its Homeland

Perhaps the most alarming and unbearable factor for any ardent, committed Muslim, especially the young, is the lack of adherence to the teachings of Islam in Muslim countries where perversion, corruption, and falsehood are rampant. Marxism and secularism are being propagated openly and publicly. The contemporary "crusaders" plan and act to in-

---

[47] Reported by al Bukhārī.

filtrate everywhere without fear. The media, in addition to clubs and theaters, spreads obscenities and misconduct. Half-naked, drunken women roam the streets tempting and provoking; drinking alcohol is legally available and common. Every aspect of distraction or sensual entertainment in the form of obscene literature, songs, plays, films, and pornographic material is being designed to corrupt and to deepen ignorance of Islam and to hamper faith.

In addition, the committed Muslim observes daily that the legislation—which is supposed to embody the beliefs and values of the Ummah in the forms of laws upholding its morals and punish those who transgress—endorses all that is forbidden by Sharī'ah and advocates corruption, because existing legislation does not derive from divine guidance but from secular philosophies. No wonder, then, that it sanctions as lawful what Allah (SWT) has prohibited and prohibits what He has made permissible. It also neglects obligations ordained by Allah (SWT) and renders the specific punishments assigned to prohibited deeds by Allah (SWT) or the Prophet (ṢA'AS) inoperative. Moreover, the young witness daily the deviation of most of the rulers of Muslim countries—those who were entrusted with this responsibility. They unashamedly make friends with the enemies of Allah (SWT) and show hostility and enmity towards those who fear Him and who endeavor to call for the divine truth; the former enjoy the rulers' favoritism and protection, the latter their wrath and oppression. Islam is seldom mentioned, except on national and "religious" occasions to deceive and beguile the masses.

Furthermore, the young constantly witness clear social injustices and great disparity between the poor and the rich, between those who can hardly exist and those who waste millions on gambling and women; they see mansions which cost millions but are only occasionally—if ever—used while millions of Muslims remain unsheltered; they hear of fortunes smuggled abroad to be kept in secret foreign accounts, while millions of Muslims are content with the little that is still denied them, those who can hardly feed their children or buy medicine for the sick and old. Yet, if those who usurp oil revenues, or those who have benefited from the policy of economic cooperation with the West, or the agents of big international companies, donated but a portion of the wealth thrown away on gambling or on women, it would relieve a great deal of poverty as well as feed and shelter tens of thousands. Countless riches and public funds are being usurped in broad daylight; bribery and favoritism are deeply rooted. Those who commit these thefts always escape justice, but those who commit relatively insignificant misdeeds are harshly and severely punished. Such injustice has created bitter feelings of envy, hatred, and malice between the various sectors of the community. The advocates of destructive ideologies exploit these feelings of bitterness to kindle the fire of class struggle and social hatred, and manage to create an atmosphere where their imported alien ideologies can be accepted as alternatives. In that atmosphere the advocates of such ideologies find a large number of people willing to listen to them, not because of a rational acceptance of their ideas but as a reaction to and hatred for prevailing conditions.

There is nothing enigmatic about the root cause of this tragic condition. Islam, as a way of life, with all its comprehensiveness, vision, justice, and balance is almost absent from the scene, a stranger in its homeland. It has been removed from public life, from the economic and public affairs of the state, from legislation and from international relations, and has been cornered in a private relationship between the individual and his Lord—a situation akin to that of Christianity during the period of its decadence. Islam has been made a *dīn* without Sharī'ah, a religion without a state, a Qur'an without authority.

Islam has been made to suffer the consequences of a past alien to its own history and to its Ummah. The history of the Catholic church in the West was rampant with disasters and negative attitudes in which the church aligned itself with despotism, with unjust monarchs and feudal lords against the helpless masses. It initiated the Inquisition, which persecuted and tortured men of knowledge and new ideas; scholars and scientists were burnt alive; ignorance and aggression were forced on societies in the name of religion, i.e., of Christianity. It is no wonder then that the masses revolted against it and sought to liberate themselves. There is no reason, however, that Islam should bear the consequences of this black and alien history, only to be banished from any influential place in legislation and in guidance of the Ummah and to be confined to the conscience of the people or to the mosque—a tongue-tied "mosque" which is always under secret service surveillance. Even there, Islam is not allowed to command the common good and forbid that which is evil and undesirable.

The problem can basically be attributed to the imposition on Muslim societies of secularism—an alien trend which is at odds with all that is Islamic. Secularism teaches the separation between religion and the state, legislation and authority—a concept unknown throughout the history of the Muslim Ummah. Islam and the Sharī'ah were always the source of *'ibādah*, of legislation, public transaction, traditions, and ethics. True, there were a few cases in which the rulers and their subjects deviated from the right path, but there was not a single incident in which Sharīʿah was neglected in settling disputes or differences between opposing parties. Even the most despotic rulers, such as al Ḥajjāj ibn Yūsuf, did not have the impudence to reject a verdict based on the Qur'ān and Sunnah. This distinction is important, because there is a tremendous difference between deviating from Sharīʿah for personal ends, envy, negligence, anger, etc., and denying its superiority over other systems; for Sharīʿah should overrule everyone and everbody by virture of its nature and capacity as embodying Allah's word and judgment: "Do they seek after a judgement of [the days of] ignorance? But who, for a people whose faith is assured, can give better judgment than Allah?" (5:50).

No wonder then that the conscience of this generation of young Muslims—confronted with this state of affairs—is shocked to find that non-Muslim countries adapt their lives in accordance with their ideologies, philosophies, or concepts about faith, existence, God, and man; yet the Muslim alone is coerced to undergo a conflict between his beliefs and his reality, between his *dīn* and his society. In this respect, I wrote:

> Secularism may be accepted in a Christian society but it can never enjoy a general acceptance in an Islamic society. Christianity is devoid of a shari'ah or a comprehensive system of life to which its adherents should be committed. The New Testament itself divides life into two parts: one for God, or religion, the other for Caesar, or the state: "Render unto Caesar things which belong to Caesar, and render unto God things which belong to God" (Mathew 22:21). As such, a Christian could accept secularism without any qualms of conscience. Furthermore, Westerners, especially Christians, have good reasons to prefer a secular regime to a religious one. Their experience with "religious regimes"—as they knew them—meant the rule of the clergy, the despotic authority of the Church, and the resulting decrees of excommunication and the deeds of forgiveness, i.e., letters of indulgence.
>
> For Muslim societies, the acceptance of secularism means something totally different; i.e., as Islam is a comprehensive system of worship *(ʿibādah)* and legislation (Sharīʿah), the acceptance of secularism means abandonment of Sharīʿah, a denial of the divine guidance and a rejection of Allah's in-

junctions; It is indeed a false claim that Sharī'ah is not proper to the requirements of the present age. The acceptance of a legislation formulated by humans means a preference of the humans' limited knowledge and experiences to the divine guidance: "Say! Do you know better than Allah?" (2:140).

For this reason, the call for secularism among Muslims is atheism and a rejection of Islam. Its acceptance as a basis for rule in place of Sharī'ah is downright *riddah*. The silence of the masses in the Muslim world about this deviation has been a major transgression and a clear-cut instance of disobedience which have produced a sense of guilt, remorse, and inward resentment, all of which have generated discontent, insecurity, and hatred among committed Muslims because such deviation lacks legality. Secularism is compatible with the Western concept of God which maintains that after God had created the world, He left it to look after itself. In this sense, God's relationship with the world is like that of a watchmaker with a watch: he makes it then leaves it to function without any need for him. This concept is inherited from Greek philosophy, especially that of Aristotle who argued that God neither controls nor knows anything about the world. This is a helpless God as described by Will Durant. There is no wonder that such a God leaves people to look after their own affairs. How can He legislate for them when He is ignorant of their affairs? This concept is totally different from that of Muslims. We Muslims believe that Allah (SWT) is the sole Creator and Sustainer of the Worlds. One Who "...takes account of every single thing" (72:28); that He is omnipotent and omniscient; that His mercy and bounties encompasses everyone and suffice for all. In that capacity, Allah (SWT) revealed His divine guidance to humanity, made certain things permissible and others prohibited, commanded people observe His injunctions and to judge according to them. If they do not do so, then they commit *kufr*, aggression, and transgression.[48]

Devout and committed young Muslims daily witness all these evil

[48] *Al Ḥulūl al Mustawradah wa Kayfa Janat 'alā Ummatīna* ("How the Imported Solutions Disastrously Affected Our Ummah"), Cairo, Wahbah Bookshop, 1977, pp. 113-114.

abominable, and un-Islamic practices, but do not know how to confront them. They cannot change things by physical force or by voicing their concern and opinion. The only way for them is to condemn these practices in their hearts, though this is the least manifestation of *īmān*. But this internal tumult cannot be suppressed forever, and must eventually explode.

In addition to all this, the Muslim world and all that Muslims hold sacrosanct are under attack. Various non-Islamic powers – Zionist, Christian, Marxist, pagan and so on, which forget their fundamental differences and join forces in an open – or covert – campaign against any signs of an Islamic revival or any form of an Islamic movement or state. For this reason, all non-Islamic issues find material and moral support from the East and the West. But Islamic issues find no real or practical support from this or that camp. Allah (SWT) has referred to such in His book: "The unbelievers are protectors, one of another" (8:73).

It is impossible for a Muslim to observe with silence and indifference the tragic mishaps that beset his Ummah, (or to watch his brothers in Islam being slaughtered like animals, or converted to Christianity, or misled into falsehood and ignorance). What about Muslim brotherhood and the solidarity of Muslims? A Muslim must believe in the brotherhood of Muslims. He should be proud of belonging to the best Ummah that has ever evolved for mankind. Futhermore, he must believe that Muslims, irrespective of their nationalities or language, are one Ummah in which the person who is least in rank is responsible for all and where all join together in solidarity against the enemy, and accept the Prophet's ḥadīth that "he who does not concern himself with the affairs of Muslims is not a Muslim". Daily news brings to the concerned Muslim reports of the sufferings of his fellow Muslims in Palestine, Lebanon, Afghanistan, the Philippines, Eritrea, Somalia, Cyprus, India or other places where either an oppressed Muslim minority or a subjugated Muslim majority exist. In addition, the young observe with indignation that such happenings do not elicit any adequate response from the governments of other Muslim countries. Instead they are completely indifferent to the persecution of fellow Muslims and they either impose a blackout on such news or, even worse, side with the enemies of Islam. The concern of Muslim rulers is for their parochial, regional, national, or racial interests, or loyalty to certain foreign powers rather than loyalty to Allah (SWT), His Prophet (ṢAʿAS), His *dīn*, His Ummah and its cause.

Muslim youth are also aware that all of these negative attitudes towards Islamic causes – locally and internationally – are initiated by foreign forces, and carried out by some Muslim rulers who act are mere puppets manipulated by Zionist, Christian, or atheist powers. These forces initiate a sense of fear in the hearts of these rulers about an Islamic revolt, convince them of a potential danger, and incite them to crush the Islamic groups or movement—they always fall into the trap!

One of the main issues that has created frustration and resentment in the minds and hearts of the young Muslims during the last two decades is the 1967 Six-Day War between Arabs and Israel—a major catastrophe whose impact was intentionally minimized when those responsible for it, as well as their accomplices, called it "the set-back" insted of "defeat". The young Muslims in Arab countries were brought up with the conviction that Israel was a parasite, an alien to the area, created by aggression and usurpation, and that the liberation of Muslim land from this foreign body was a national and religious obligation; that Israel had no right to occupy a land that did not belong to it. The late Ḥāj Amīn al Ḥusaynī (RA), muftī of Palestine, said in this regard: "Palestine is not a country without a people to accept a homeless people!" However, after the catastrophic defeat of the Arab regimes in 1967, politics in the Arab world took a new turn whose main objective became "the reparation of the effects of the aggression," i.e., recognition of the existence of Israel. In fact, this means that the 1967 Israeli aggression has legalized the previous ones. If that is so, then what was the reason for the 1949, 1956, and 1967 wars? Why did the Arab regimes not agree to recognize Israel from the beginning and relieve the Ummah of the tragic consequences of these wars? This was followed by the "initiative" of the so-called "peaceful solution" and peace treaties. But such an endeavor was disappointing and frustrating to the aspirations of Muslim youth. The authorities in Egypt tried to justify these on military and political, local as well as international, considerations. But all this was a severe shock to the hopes and the aspirations of Muslim youth. The shock was augmented by the fact that all of the major powers supported the illegal existence of Israel although the rights of the Arabs and Muslims were obvious. This led to the inevitable conclusion—supported by authentic evidence—especially among the youth, that a contemporary "crusade" assuming a new form is being waged against Islam. These feelings greatly influenced the Muslim youth who sensed that the old crusading spirit still motivated a large number of Western politicians and leaders who view the whole Islamic world, as well as any Islamic movement, with inherited hatred accumulated through centuries of struggle with the Muslim Ummah.

Many Muslim intellectuals, however, very much doubted the reality of this Western crusading spirit, claiming that national interests are paramount and are usually the sole motives for the West when taking a political or a military decision or action. But recent and current circumstances have clearly demonstrated to these optimists that they have been wrong and that the crusading spirit is still alive. I am not speaking of Generals Allenby or Gourand but of our own contemporaries: Why does the West support Israel to exist on Muslim land? Why does the United States challenge the whole world by vetoing every United Nations resolution that condemns Israel? Why does it support Ethiopia—though a Marxist country for many years—against Eritrea? Why is there a blackout on all Muslim causes, yet a great deal of fuss is made about far lesser incidents, i.e. the hijacking of an airplane? Why is the Muslim blood cheaper than that of others? There seems to be no explanation for this other than the existence of a devilish alliance of Zionist, Christian, and atheist powers for a vicious and united campaign against Islam and Muslims.

In the opinion of devout young Muslims, all the rulers of the Arab and Muslim countries are mere "pieces on a chessboard" and puppets in the hands of the secret powers which rule the world. They see military coups d'état and major political changes in the Muslim world as mere maneuvers by foreign powers to bring to office persons who are incapable of managing anything, but are made to appear as heroes. There may be some exaggeration in all this, but on the whole, the suspicions of the young are partly well-founded and supported by many events and incidents which strongly establish the conviction that the rulers are accomplices in a devilish strategy which seeks to nip the Islamic reawakening in the bud. The youth strongly believe that these rulers only appear to be true national leaders concerned for their people and their religion, while in reality they are no more than paid agents serving the enemies of the Ummah.

9. The Impediments Imposed on *Da'wah* and *Du'āh*

Another cause of extremism pertains to the freedom—indeed duty—to call people to Islam. It is a truism that Islam teaches a person not only to be pious and righteous but also to endeavor to reform others. This is the purpose of the obligation to call people to righteousness, to command the common good and forbid that which is evil and undesirable, to join together in mutual teaching of truth and of patience. From the Islamic point of view, every Muslim is required to call to Islam to the best of his or her ability. The following verse is addressed to every Muslim: "Invite [all] to the Way of your Lord. . ." (16:125). Furthermore, every follower of the Prophet (ṢA'AS) is a *dā'iyah*, as the following verse makes clear: "Say: This is my way. I invite unto Allah – with evidence as clear as the seeing with one's eyes – I and whoever follows me" (12:108). Henceforth, the motto of the reformers: "Make yourself righteous, and call others to righteousness." The Qur'ān says: "Who is better in speech than one who calls [men] to Allah, works righteousness, and says, 'I am of those who bow in Islam'" (41:33).

Islam does not want a Muslim to work alone. The Prophet (ṢA'AS) said: "Allah's hand [of support] is with the group," and also: "A believer to another believer like a building whose different bricks enforce one another."[49] Cooperation in kindness and in commanding righteousness is not only a religious obligation but a vital necessity. It is no wonder, therefore, that collective work in the field of *da'wah* is an obligatory duty, because that without which a *wājib* (obligation) cannot otherwise be completed is in itself a *wājib.* The fact that non-Muslim ideological forces work collectively in the form of blocs, parties, and associations makes it incumbent upon Muslims to counter these forces by similar techniques. Otherwise, we will continue to lag behind, totally unable to do anything while others achieve progress. For this reason, the gravest sins committed by some of the governments in Muslim countries are the censorship of the freedom to call people to Islam as a *dīn* and a system of beliefs and a way of life, and the intimidation of *du'āh* and those who call for the application of Sharī'ah, the establishment of the Islamic state, the unity of the Ummah, the liberation of Muslim land, and the support of all Islamic causes. This pressure on *da'wah* and *du'āh*, and the restriction of all forms of Islamic work, especially the collective one, is one of the main causes that generates extremism. This is especially so since the adherents of secular philosphies and ideologies are allowed to organize themselves in groups and to disseminate their ideas with complete freedom and support and without any interference or restriction. It is illogical to grant complete freedom – in Muslim land – to the advocates of secularism, Marxism, liberalism, and so on, to establish parties,

---

[49] Reported by al Bukhārī.

organizations, newspapers, and magazines, and alone censor Islam and its *du'āh,* who speak for the majority of the people.

Da'wah to Islam, as a positive and comprehensive *dīn* and a way of life, faces censorship and suppression in many Muslim countries. The only form of Islam allowed is that upheld by the dervishes and the professional traders in religion; the "Islam" of the ages of backwardness and decadence; the "Islam" which only celebrates occasions, supports despotic rulers, and prays for them to have a "long life." It is an "Islam" based on "Divine pre-determination" and "no-choice" in belief, sanctions Islamically condemmed *bid'a* (innovation) in *'ibādah* (worship), permits passive ethics and intellectual rigidity, and encourages emphasis on minor rather than major and vital issues. Those who follow and promote this "Islam" are patronized by corrupt and despotic rulers. Even the irreligious, secularist rulers bless this form of religiosity, show respect and support to its advocates in order to enable them to lull the deprived masses and induce them to the status quo, and engage the youth in a web of illusions, symbols, terms, and trivialities. In this way, they sabotage their zeal for *jihād*, their determination to fight against injustice, perversion, and corruption. Perhaps this is what led Marx to claim that "religion is the opiate of the people."

But the authentic original Islam, which is contained in the Qur'ān and the *Sunnah*—understood and practiced by the companions of the Prophet (ṢA'AS) as well as the *Tābi'ūn*—as the embodiment of truth and power, honor and dignity, sacrifice and *jihād*, is—as we have mentioned earlier—rejected by those in authority because it kindles the spirit of revolt against injustice and darkness, and teaches its adherents to emulate the practice of ". . .those who preach the messages of Allah and fear Him, and fear none but Allah" (33:39).

In this conviction and clarity of vision, they believe that since sustenance and the duration of a person's life are determined by Allah alone, there is no reason to fear or to seek support from anyone except Him. In contemporary Turkey, a Muslim country, which had been the headquarters of the caliphate for several centuries, the leader of a popular party—who was deputy premier at the time—was led from his ministry into prison. He and his followers were brought to court, accused of calling for the application of the Sharī'ah in a country where 98% of the population are Muslims! The prosecution brought fifteen charges against them, all of which centered on their endeavor to change Turkey from an irreligious secular state that opposed Islam (the religion of the Turkish people) to a state that respects its religion and abides by its injunctions, as is consistent with the requirements of *īmān*. The military authority which rules Turkey by force pledges obedience to Ataturk (Muṣṭafā Kamāl), the founder of secular Turkey, rather than to Allah (SWT) and His Prophet (ṢA'AS). Consequently, it regards any call for the application of Sharī'ah or the return to the Islamic way of life as a crime, even if the caller uses legal means which are acknowledged and sanctioned by all "democratic systems," one which the authorities enjoy praising. These devoted Muslims were not prosecuted for using force and violence to topple the government, but simply because they believed in Islam—the faith of their fathers and forefathers—and sought to call to it by wisdom and amicability through legal platforms and constitutional channels. The military prosecutor accused them of raising the following slogans: "Islam is the only course," "Muḥammad (ṢA'AS) is the sole leader," "Sharī'ah and Islam are one and the same," and "The Qur'ān is the constitution."

Is it possible for any Muslim—who accepts Allah (SWT) as his Lord, Islam as his *dīn*, and Muḥammad (ṢA'AS) as his Prophet—to deny these? What could Muslims who aspire to live in accordance with the teachings of Islam do while *kufr* is prescribed and *'īmān* is rejected; while *ḥarām* is made lawful and *ḥalal* unlawful? Are these not unnatural situations the root cause of excessiveness and extremism?

In one of the Afro-Arab countries which is considered part of "the Free World," the communists are permitted to establish an official political party which engages in open activities and is protected by the constitution and laws of that country. But the Islamic trend which represents the real conscience of the nation, its beliefs, suffering, and aspirations, is prohibited from having a legal, official existence or platform. Worse, all Islamic leaders and active *du'āt* in that country are in prison and are being subjected to the most atrocious and heinous punishments. The only charge against them is that they declare that only Allah (SWT) is their Lord, that Truth is their ultimate goal, that Islam is the only course and source of judgment, that the word is their weapon, and that knowledge is their only provision.

Is it logical, therefore, to blame the youth who—despairing of being allowed to call for Islam with wisdom and nice preaching—have resorted to other means through which they can meet force by force and violence by violence. This situation should not be allowed to continue. Islam will, *in shā'a Allāh*, find followers and supporters and a party of believers who continue to be committed to the Truth, unimpaired and unhampered by those who oppose them or those who let them down. It is in our interest to acknowledge our responsibility to let this party of believers be naturally born and give them a chance to mature and develop in a healthy atmosphere of freedom and a way from oppression or pressure; otherwise, events will take a different course unacceptable to us. *Da'wah* to Islam and to the way of Allah (SWT) will burst forth, and unless it is given the chance to be open, without any restrictions and hinderances, underground covert activities will be attempted, which usually cause confusion and lead to extremism.

The gravest mistake of the authorities is resorting to violence, physical as well as psychological torture in prisons and concentration camps, where humans are treated as animals. In Egypt (both in 1954 as well as 1965), devout Muslims were subjected to nightmarish, frightening, unbelievable torture and punishment at the Military Prison near Cairo: they were lashed, exposed to flames, their flesh burnt with cigarettes; men, and sometimes even women, were hung upside down like slaughtered animals, while the executioners took turns scorching them until their bodies swelled up in heaps of blood and pus. Many were martyred in this beastial way while their executioners showed no fear of Allah (SWT) and showed no mercy or humanity. They not only used all the forms of torture engineered by Nazism, Fascism, and Communism, but also innovated and developed new techniques.

Extremism and the tendency for *takfīr* were born in this notorious prison. The prisoners began by asking simple questions: Why are we subjected to this torture? What crime have we committed? Have we said anything other than that Allah (SWT) is our Lord, Islam is our path, and the Qur'ān is our constitution? In so doing, we seek nothing but Allah's pleasure. We have not sought any reward or thanks from anybody! Could commitment to the cause of Islam in a Muslim country be regarded as a crime for which we are being tortured in this way? These questions led to others: Who are these beasts who torture us, degrade our humanity, curse our religion, dishonor our sacred beliefs, mock our religious devotions and *'ibādah*, and even dare to disrespect our God? One of their high-ranking officials once said: "Bring me your God and I will put him in jail." Could these be regarded as Muslims? What is *kufr* if these are Muslims? There is no doubt that these are *kuffār* who must be expelled from the fold of Islam.

This in turn led to further questions: If this is our judgment of those who torture us to death, what should our judgment of their masters be? What judgment should be made against the leaders and rulers in authority who not only refuse to rule in accordance with Allah's injunctions but also wage war against those who call for the application of His Sharī'ah.

In comparison with the former, the latter are worse in their *kufr* and more categorical in their *riddah* as described in the Qur'ān: "If any fail to judge by [the light of] what Allah has revealed, they are [no better than] unbelievers" (5:44). Having come to this conclusion, these oppressed Muslims raised a further question addressed to their fellow inmates: What do you think of the rulers who do not judge in accordance with what Allah (SWT) has revealed, and who torture those who call for the application of His Sharī'ah? Those who agreed with them that such rulers are *kuffār* were regarded as friends; those who did were considered not as enemies, even as *kuffār*, claiming that he who holds any doubt about the *kufr* of a *kāfir* is himself a *kāfir*. But that was not all. Another question was raised about the people who submit to and obey such rulers. The answer was ready: they are also *kuffār* like their rulers, because—it was claimed—he who submits to a *kāfir* is himself a *kāfir*.

In this way the tendency to label individuals and groups with *kufr* was born and nurtured. The observable fact is that violence not only breeds violence but also contaminates clear thinking; suppression inevitably causes revolt.

CHAPTER THREE

Toward a Remedy for Extremism

After throwing light on the so-called "religious extremism," pointing out aspects of its true nature and characteristics and revealing its most important causes, motives, and stimulants, we now need to outline a remedy for it, its means, and methods. It should be emphasized at the outset that the remedy is inseparable from the causes and must, therefore, be as varied and complex as the causes themselves are. Needless to say, no magical touch can put an end to extremism or bring back the extremists to the line of moderation. The malaise afflicting the soul and mind of mankind is far more deeply rooted than we think, and consequently more difficult to treat. Extremism is essentially a religious phenomenon with a variety of psychological, social, and political dimensions. As such, all of these aspects must be tackled from an Islamic point of view.

I do not agree with the determinists who hold either society alone or the prevailing economic conditions responsible for the causes of the phenomenon, while they ignore the actions and behavior of the young, whom they consider to be totally helpless. It is unjust to hold the young alone responsible and to exonerate the society, the regime, and its governmental departments—especially those in charge of education, guidance, and the media. The responsibility is in fact mutual, and each partly played an important part. The Prophet (ṢA'AS) said: "All of you are guardians and responsible for your wards and the things under your care."[1] Therefore, we intend to discuss in the following part the duties that should be played by society in order to overcome extremism, as well as the duties of the youth to resist this destructive tendency.

1. Duties of Society

I have already pointed out that the inner contradictions and the chaos which characterize present-day Muslim societies, as well as the estrangement of these societies from Islam, have significantly contributed to the birth and spread of extremism. Therefore, these societies must play a

---

[1] Reported by al Bukhārī and Muslim.

positive role in the remedy. The initial step for a Muslim society is to acknowledge and confirm its genuine commitment to Islam. This cannot be achieved through a verbal declaration or expression, or through a set of slogans or a clause in the constitution stating that "Islam is the official religion of the state," but only through true adherence to the teachings of Islam.

Islam is a comprehensive system of life. It invests its divine character in life and guides it along an ethical direction; it sets up the framework, the landmarks, and the limits which govern the movement and goals of life, always keeping it on the right path, protecting it from pitfalls or from straying. For this reason, Islam consists of beliefs which can enrich the mind, of *'ibādāt* which purify the heart, of morals which purify the soul, of legislations which establish justice, and of manners which beautify life. To be really Islamic society must commit itself to Islam in its totality, unlike the Israelites who adopted only parts of the Torah but ignored the rest. Consequently, Allah (SWT) admonished them in the Qur'ān:

> Then is it only a part of the Book that you believe in, and do you reject the rest? But what is the reward for those among you who behave like this but disgrace in this life? And on the Day of Judgment they shall be consigned to the most grievous penalty (2:85).

Furthermore, for a society to be Islamic it must be willing to apply Allah's injunctions and the *Sunnah* of His Prophet (ṢAAS) on all the affairs and aspects of life: social, economic, political, or intellectual. This is the requisite of *īmān*:

> But no, by the Lord, they can have no [real] faith, until they make you judge in all disputes between them, and find in their souls no resistance against your decisions, but accept them with the fullest conviction (4:65).

And:

> The answer of the believers, when summoned to Allah and His Messenger, in order that He may judge between them, is no other than this: they say, "We hear and we obey." It is such as these that will attain felicity (24:51).

Our societies must endeavor to eliminate this obvious contradiction—we believe in Islam both as a divine creed and a Sharī'ah, but we have abandoned its Sharī'ah and disregarded its guidance and moral teachings.

These we have replaced with imported systems and alien ideologies from both the East and the West yet we still claim to be Muslims!

Our rulers must understand and realize that they are in a Muslim land and are ruling Muslim peoples who are entitled to be governed in accordance with the teachings of their religion. Constitutions, laws, educational systems, etc., must all reflect and express the people's beliefs, values, and traditions, which must also be guided, consolidated, and disseminated via the media. The economic and social policies—at local and international levels—must be formulated within the framework of these beliefs and must serve their goals. The failure of the rulers in Muslim countries to live up to these legitimate expectations is utterly unacceptable and is in stark contradiction to Islam.

Indeed, these rulers' defiance of the conscience of Muslims in most Muslim countries has become intolerable. Some of them openly reject Islam and express their commitment to an Eastern or a Western ideology. Moreover, they deprive Islam of any form of expression. Even the mosque and its religious activities are manipulated to express support for regimes and rulers. Those who dare to object are harshly and severely punished. Other rulers in Muslim countries profess to be Muslims, but their concept of Islam is a version of their own coinage and satanic whims. They pick and choose, accepting that which serves their own egotistic pursuit, and discarding that which does not appeal to them! What they themselves "believe" and declare to be "Islamic" is the "truth," and what they reject is "*bāṭil*." In this contention, they disregard all the interpretations of the venerable forebears, as well as their renowned successors and contemporaries. They unscrupulously disagree with the whole Ummah, ignoring the established traditions of the companions of the Prophet (ṢA'AS), the jurists, the interpreters of the Qur'ān and Hadith. They see no need or reason to consult any of these. Such a ruler considers himself to be a *faqīh*, an interpreter, a narrator, a *mutakallim*, and a philosopher.

Such a ruler claims to be that one man to whom there is no second. He does not see any need to learn anything even from the Prophet Muḥammad (ṢA'AS) himself, claiming that he relies on the Qur'ān alone, forgetting that the Prophet (ṢA'AS) is the interpreter of the Qur'ān. In this respect Allah (SWT) says: "He who obeys the Messenger, obeys Allah" (4:80). Nevertheless, some of these rulers allow the operation of Sharī'ah pertaining only to private affairs, as well as insignificant opportunities for talks about Islam on the radio and on television; they also permit a column in a daily newspaper to appear on Fridays only. Its theme—if any—is confined to religion in its Western Christian conception as a relationship between the conscience of the individual and his Creator. It has nothing to do with either society or life; Caesar and the Lord each gets that which belongs to him! Theirs is the concept of "religion" as "faith" without Sharī'ah, a "*dīn*" without an Islamic state, private "*'ibādah*" without any *da'wah*, *jihād*, or an obligation to command the common good and prohibit evil and the undesirable. If a person condemns something as wrong, criticizes certain deviations, advocates a call for the right path, confronts *bāṭil*, either from the platform of a mosque or in a newspaper, he is harshly reminded that he has exceeded all bounds by mixing religion and politics! For such rulers there is neither a place for religion in politics, nor politics in religion. All this contradicts, of course, the teachings of Allah (SWT) and the *Sunnah* of His Prophet (ṢA'AS), as well as the practices of the companions and *Tābi'ūn*. It is indeed high time for our rulers to realize that there can neither be stability in their societies nor hope for their peoples except through real commitment and adherence to Islam. 'Umar ibn al Khaṭṭāb (RA'A) said: "We had been the lowest of nations, but Allah honored us with Islam. Should we try to attain honor through means other than Islam, Allah will debase us." Furthermore, unless Sharī'ah is applied, our societies will continue to breed extremists, religious or otherwise.

The second step of the remedy pertains to the attitude of the Society towards the youth. To begin with, we—the old—must not address them from ivory towers, showing a superiority or a disregard for them. This attitude is bound to create a deep rift which will force them to refuse to trust or listen to us. Equally, we must not fail to understand them or to have insight into the deep recesses of their lives and the reality of their concerns. Our attitude towards them should not only be that of accusation mainly concerned with publicizing their demerits, exaggerating their negative characteristics and suspecting and discrediting their intentions and actions in an endeavor to prove them eligible for the most severe punishments. On the contrary, we should first and foremost treat them with paternal and brotherly love, making them feel that they are a part of us, our beloved ones, and the hope of the future of the Ummah. Through love and compassion, rather than through accusations and arrogance, we can come nearer to them. We should stand in their defense since allegations from all directions are raised against them—true and false, well-meaning and malicious. If we cannot assume the role of the defender, for one reason or another, we should at least stand firmly for the application of justice, which neither punishes without evidence nor sides with either the claimant or the defendant.

One of our defects is our tendency to make hasty, generalized final and conclusive judgments on social issues. This is often done without listening to the defense of the accused or the evidence cited—an attitude devoid of any sense of justice. Many people rush to judge these youth without actually knowing them, without mixing with them in order to find out how they think, feel, behave, and react. Many judge them all through the behavior of a few, despite the fact that the majority cannot be held responsible for the deeds and behavior of the minority. It is for this reason that Muslim jurists legislated that the judgment passed on the majority is binding on the whole but not vice versa. Furthermore, some people pass final judgments on a person on the basis of one single instance of behavior for which he may have had his own motives and specific personal circumstances. If his accusers but listen patiently to his justifications, they may change their minds. In any case, no final, changing moral judgement should be passed on a person on the basis of one or two actions. A person should—in the light of the following Qur'ānic verse—be evaluated on the basis of the totality of his actions and behavior: "Then those whose balance [of good deeds] is heavy, they will attain salvation" (23:102).

On the other hand, there are people who judge the youth through their own personal conception of what religion is and what it means to be religious. In the opinion of such people, these youth Muslims are merely eccentrics suffering from psychological problems. This may be true of a small number, but on the whole the youth are psychologically sound, the sincerity of their deeds is unquestionable—their private and public practice and performance are, indeed, harmonious. They are free from any dichotomy between belief and practice, between what they publicly profess and what they cherish in their hearts. I myself have known very well many of these young Muslims in many Muslim countries; I bear witness that I found strength in their *īmān*, firmness in their convictions, truth in their words, and sincerity in their work. I also admire their love for the truth and hatred of *bāṭil*, their ardor for disseminating the divine message, their determination to command the common good and forbid evil and the undesirable, their zeal for *jihād*, their concern for Muslims everywhere in the world, their aspiration for the establishment of an Islamic society which lives in accordance with the teachings of Allah (SWT), is guided by Islam, and disciplined by Sharī'ah and its ethical values.

My meetings and contacts with these youth have convinced me of the tremendous differences between our traditional Islamic conception and theirs; they are committed to a new vital Islam which opposes our own worn-out traditional belief. Their *'īmān* is warm and ardent while ours is cold; their determination to righteousness is solid and unflinching while ours is apathetic; their hearts fear Allah (SWT) and are full of love for Him—their hearts beat with His remembrance in their constant recitation of the Qur'ān. One must also acknowledge their determination to recapture the true Islamic spirit and to reconstruct life according to it. I know that many of them spend whole nights in *'ibādah*, offer *ṣiyām* during the day, ask Allah's forgiveness at dawn, and emulate good deeds. It is for this reason that many people, including myself, entertain the hope that the future of Islam will, in *shā'a Allāh*, be realized through the determined endeavors of these youths. This is why I have declared on several occasions in Egypt that the young generation who grew up in righteousness and piety is the real treasure upon which Egypt could build its hopes. They are more valuable than any material considerations.

I equally believe that whoever tries to suggest a remedy for this issue must show balance, justice, and open-mindedness. Otherwise, such a person is himself bound to display extremism while discussing the phenomenon and suggesting its remedy. The first characteristic of balance in this regard is to avoid exaggerating the manifestations of the alleged phenomenon, making much fuss about nothing, thereby spreading fright and terror. This, unfortunately, is our customary tendency in dealing with such issues. Exaggeration is extremely damaging because it distorts the facts, upsets the criteria of judgment, blurs vision, and contaminates clear thinking. Consequently, any verdict for or against the issue is bound to be either unjust or, at least, incomplete.

It is regrettable that a great deal of what has been or is being said or written in the aftermath of the crisis resulting from the authorities' clash with the Muslim youth in Egypt and the emergence of so-called "religious extremism" is not free from exaggeration and excessiveness in the attempt to tackle the issue. These attempts are influenced by the inconducive, ill-willed atmosphere shared by the majority of people against the youth. This attitude provoked the Egyptian sociologist, Dr. Sā'd al Dīn Ibrāhīm, who observed their phenomenon to respond to this campaign directed against the youth in an article published in *al Ahrām* newspaper. Dr. Ibrāhīm pointed out that those who have taken part in analyzing this issue are actually ignorant of its rudiments.

Indeed, it would have been more proper if these people had kept silent or had approached the subject with truth and fairness, examining the phenomenon in a realistic and balanced manner. But this requires qualities which these people do not possess. A balanced opinion would take into consideration the fact that religious extremism is often a reaction to another opposing extremism such as permissiveness and laxity in religious matters or cynical attitudes towards religion. Therefore there should be an attempt to bring both extremes to the moderation of Islam. The very nature of living occasionally sets one form of extremism against another in order to create a balance, a concept found in the Qur'ān:

And did not Allah check one set of people by means of another, the earth would indeed be full of mischief: But Allah is full of bounty to all the worlds (2:251).

Strangely enough the extremist Muslim youth are unfairly treated but other extremist groups—especially those who lead an immoral and totally irreligious life—are not condemned. Nor are such people ever imprisoned or subjected to harsh punishments. Justice requires that both types of extremism be condemned.

Is it fair then to put all the blame on and direct our vexation at the youth who live for and in accordance with the teachings of Islam—those who regularly perform their *ṣalāh*, eschew prohibitions, lower their gaze, and guard their modesty and chastity; those who carefully investigate what is lawful and what is prohibited; those who adhere adamantly to what they believe to be an Islamic norm of behavior—such as growing a beard, wearing above-the-ankle clothes, using mouth-cleaning *siwāk*; those who avoid vain talk, who never smoke, and prudently spend their money on what is useful? Is it fair to condemn these young people who have grown up in piety and righteousness, however excessive and strict they may be, while we keep silent about the immorally permissive behavior of others among whom it is hard to distinguish between the "male" and the "female"? Morally as well as intellectually Westernized, the latter have been completely uprooted from Muslim culture. Is it fair to make so much fuss about and condemn so-called "religious extremism" and yet keep silent about "irreligious extremism"? Is it fair to disparage and sneer at a young woman who veils her face because she is convinced that her action is in tune with Islamic teachings and through which she seeks Allah's acceptance, and yet keep silent about another who walks about in the streets or seashores or appears on television or movies almost naked, deliberately seeking to provoke the instincts, claiming that she is simply exercising "personal freedom" which is sanctioned by the constitution? Do constitutions provide for "personal freedom" with regard to nakedness and banality but prohibit it with regard to modesty and chastity?

If society had stood against those who were immoral and irreligious and had endeavored to change all the manifestations of evil, the phenomenon of "religious extremism" would never have existed in our countries. Even if it could have appeared—for one reason or another—its impact would have been less significant than it is at present. We also need to acknowledge that extremism is universal, manifesting itself in various ways and areas, such as religion, politics, thought and behavior.

There are indeed many very active non-Muslim religious extremist groups; they have neither been condemned by the world—as Muslim groups have been—nor have they been treated by their countries as the Muslim groups have been in theirs. We have seen Jewish religious extremism in Zionist Israel, being embodied in parties and organizations that declared their principles and aims without any fear or shame. Moreover, the Zionist state, formed by ursurping a Muslim land, was ideologically based on religious extremism and deduced from Jewish Scriptures and the Talmud, as well as from their belief to be God's chosen people and the divine masters of the world, and that violence is lawful for them to achieve their goals. The Christian *katāʾib* ("Falangists") groups in Lebanon similarly exercise extreme forms of violence and practice religious extremism; they slaughter Muslims, mutilate their bodies, cut off their private parts and put them in their mouths, assault Muslim women, burn Muslim religious books (including the Qur'ān), and seek to degrade everything related to Islam and Muslims—all this being done in the name of Christianity and Christ, the Apostle of peace and love, who addressed his followers: "Love your enemies, do good to those who hate you, bless those who curse you . . . if anyone hits you on the right cheek, let him hit the other one too" (Luke 6:27-29).

Moreover, we have witnessed many forms of Christian religious extremism all directed against the Muslims, not only in Lebanon, but also in Cyprus, Eritrea, the Philippines, as well as in other places and countries. It matters little whether it is Catholic extremism, Orthodox extremism, or Protestant extremism; it is Christian extremism—a new Crusade.

Furthermore, almost every year extremist Hindu religions groups massacre many innocent and peaceful Muslims. The irony is that those who slaughter human beings in cold blood prohibit the slaughter of animals because they claim it is cruel and merciless to kill a living creature! For this same reason, they do not kill mice but allow them to eat up the wheat that grows in millions of acres. All of these creatures, they claim, should not be harmed because they have "souls"! But these people never hesitate to slaughter Muslims, as if the latter were the only beings devoid of souls!

In addition to all this we have to realize that we live in an age of uneasiness, anxiety, and rebellion generated by the spread of a materialism which has twisted human thought and behavior. Although man has succeeded in landing on the moon, he has failed miserably to realize his happiness on earth. It is obvious that the twentieth century has witnessed rapid progress in all the fields of science, a development which only brought about material – not spiritual – prosperity. This, however, has not been able to create the happiness and peace of mind for which so many of its beneficiaries had hoped. On the contrary, it has caused an ever-increasing number of people – like the hippies – to feel lost and confused, and to rebel against this "modernization" by going back to nature. For them, life has no meaning, and civilization has failed to answer their persistent questions: Who am I? What is my message? Where did I come from and to where am I going? Such anxiety and rebellion found an echo in our countries as well, where it led either to irreligiosity or to a greater commitment and adherence to Islam. Some young Muslims found the answers to their questions in Islam and therefore turned to it with warmth and often with excessive zeal.

It would be unreasonable to expect peace and tranquility in the present age of rebellion, or moderation and balance in a world characterized by extremism. Nor would it be logical to demand from these enthusiastic young people the "wisdom and maturity" of their elders. Man is, in a sense, a product of his environment.

The secret services must abandon their harsh methods, torture, and assassinations. We must spread and encourage an atmosphere of freedom, welcome criticism, and reactivate the practice of our forebears in advising each other. We have an example of this in the practice and the following words of 'Umar ibn al Khaṭṭāb: "May Allah bless the person who points out my faults to me." Hence he always encouraged and supported those who advised or criticized him.

One day while he was with a group of his companions, a man said to him: "O, Caliph, fear Allah..." 'Umar's companions were angered by this, but he asked them to let the man express himself freely, saying: "There is no good in you if you do not speak up (like this man), and there is no good in us (the rulers) if we do not listen (to your advice and criticism)."

On another occasion, 'Umar addressed his audience: "If any of you sees any deviation in me, it is his duty to put it right." Upon hearing this, a bedouin stood up and said: "By Allah, if we see any deviation in you, we will put it right with our swords (i.e., even if we have to use force)," 'Umar was not angered, but was pleased enough to say: "*Al Ḥamdu li Allāh* that there are Muslims ready to use their swords to put 'Umar on the right path."

An atmosphere of freedom produces ideas which can be rationally discussed and analyzed by the learned, either to be adapted and adopted or to be discarded and rejected and eventually disappear. Otherwise ideas are bound to thrive secretly, to be nurtured covertly, and to eventually take roots, develop and grow until they become dominant and strong, taking people by surprise because they were neither aware of their birth nor development. Deviant thought and understanding are the sources of extremism, and sound thought and correct understanding must therefore be utilized in its treatment. It is indeed a grave mistake to resort to power to counter deviant thought; confused thoughts must be carefully, patiently, and intellectually rectified. The brutal methods adopted by the secret police, by leaders of military coups who torture and kill whoever disagree with them, cannot possibly put an end to extremism. They may succeed temporarily, but they will ultimately fail in their endeavor. If one extreme group is crushed, another—even more violent—is in the making.

The first duty then is to create a rational Islamic awareness based on an enlightened *fiqh* in the teachings of Islam: a *fiqh* of deep insight which does not concentrate on the marginal issues only but on the essentials as well; a *fiqh* which relates the parts to the whole, the branches to the roots, the hypothetical to the definitive; a *fiqh* which seeks judgments from the original sources, not only from the branches. Creating such an awareness and developing such a *fiqh* among the extremist is not easy. Moreover, to change the beliefs and convictions of people needs sincere effort, great patience, and the support and guidance of Allah *ta'ālā*.

Those in authority imagine—or are led to believe—that such changes can be easily effected by the media. They think that these channels can alter the intellectual as well as the spiritual convictions of people in the direction they desire. They either unwittingly or deliberately ignore the fact that the state-controlled media and their spokesmen, agents, and agencies are incapable of actualizing the required changes and consciousness, because the form and substance of such endeavors are totally rejected by the youth. This has been attempted by various regimes in different countries where the authorities exploited some *'ulamā'* and speakers to lecture prisoners in order to brainwash them. But all these lectures, speeches, and sermons were mocked and failed miserably to achieve that end. The aspired imparting of knowledge can only be realized by *'ulamā'* who are free from the crippling influence of authority—scholars who enjoy the confidence of the youth because of the originality of their knowledge and the impeccability of their religious convictions. In addition, this requires a naturally conducive atmosphere free from the false promises and intellectual terrorism which prevail behind closed doors. Furthermore, such transformation cannot be achieved overnight through lofty inculcation and martial orders. On the contrary, it requires free encounter, constructive dialogue, and mutual communication, all of which are needed to realize this goal in the long run.

What I wish to emphasize in this respect is the danger of confronting one form of intellectual extremism with another; that is, confronting obstinacy with obstinancy, bigotry with bigotry, reacting to a misdeed with another misdeed. The danger manifests itself, for example, in a tendency to accuse of *kufr* the extremists who accuse others of being *kuffār*. Perhaps some of the people who adopt such an attitude cite the following ḥadīth as evidence of the truth of their claim: "He himself who accuses a Muslim of *kufr* commits *kufr*." The truth is that if we behave in this manner, we fall into the same pitfall. However, the ḥadīth under consideration does not include a Muslim who accuses another Muslim of *kufr* as a result of judicial misinterpretation and misunderstanding. This can be demonstrated by authentic *aḥādīth* as well as confirmed events in the lives of the companions (RA'A).

We have a good example in the attitude of the caliph 'Alī ibn Abū Ṭālib (RA'A) towards the Khawārij who fought him and unjustly accused him of the kind of repulsive abominations that could not be hurled against an ordinary Muslim, let alone 'Alī, the most renowned and courageous Muslim hero, the cousin of the Prophet (ṢA'AS) and his son-in-law. Nonetheless, 'Alī condemned the Khawārij's false and nugatory allegations without branding them *kuffār,* as they had done to him. Furthermore, he accommodated them in the fold of Islam thinking well of their intention.

Hence when the people asked 'Alī whether the Khawārij were *kuffār,* he replied: "They have escaped *kufr*...." The people persisted: "What are they then?" 'Alī answered: "Our brothers in the past who wrong us today!" This means that the Khawārij are to be judged as those committing *baghy,*[2] not as *kuffār* or *murtaddīn*. *Bughāt*—in this case—are those who do not obey a just Muslim imām on the basis of a judicial misinterpretation.

---

[2] *Al Baghy*: "False or evil endeavor, one vitiated by false/evil intention and/or consequence." (*Baghy, Bughāt* pl.)

If such people are powerful and rebel against the imām, he should not hasten to fight them, but should send to them people who can rectify their errors by arguing nicely, wisely, and patiently with them in order to prevent the shedding of Muslim blood and to preserve Muslim unity. If they persist in their attitude and initiate war, they should be fought until they abide by Allah's command. But during fighting, those of them who flee from the battlefield should not be persecuted, nor should their wounded or prisoners of war be killed, their women should not be taken captive, and their belongings should not be confiscated. They are to be treated as Muslims who are fought only because they constitute a menance to the Ummah, since the aim is not to exterminate them but to bring them back to the fold of Islam. Convictions can neither be altered by force nor by the threat of the sword.

Another instance of 'Alī's attitude is worth mentioning as evidence of the unprecedented level of the freedom of expression—especially that of the opposition—attained in the early days of Islam; a level which other countries achieved only many centuries afterwards. The Khawārij dissented because they rejected 'Alī's acceptance of arbitration claiming that: "The [command] is only Allah's." 'Alī replied to this with his laconic, proverbial saying: "This is a word of truth twisted in the service of *bāṭil*." In spite of their opposition to him, 'Alī told them clearly and frankly: "We are committed not to prevent you from *ṣalāh* in mosques, nor from your share in booty, nor to initiate fighting with you unless you create corruption in the land (of Islam)." Thus 'Alī granted the opposition—the Khawārij—all these rights, although each of them was a fully trained, armed soldier capable of taking up arms at any moment.

It is also worth pointing out in this respect that although an authentic ḥadīth describes the Khawārij as dissenters there was a consensus among the *'ulamā'* to refrain from branding them as *kuffār*, and sanctioned fighting and killing them, and although they themselves have branded all Muslims *kuffār*. Al Imām al Shawkānī says in *Nayl al Awṭār*:[3]

> Most of the Sunni jurists are of the opinion that the Khawārij are Muslims on the basis of their witnessing that there is no God but Allah and that Muḥammad is His Messenger, and their regular observance of the other pillars of Islam. Their sinfulness is the result of a reliance on an erroneous interpretation on the basis of which they held all other Muslims to be *kuffār*. This led them to proscribe their

[3] *Nayl al Awṭār*, 7:352-353.

opponents and to openly accuse them of *kufr* and polytheism.

Al Khaṭābī says:

> Although the Khawārij have strayed from the right path, Muslim *'ulamā'* are unanimously agreed that they are an Islamic group. Therefore they have permitted intermarriage with them and eating the animals they slaughter. Furthermore they should not be considered *kuffār* as long as they continue to adhere to the fundamentals of Islam.

'Iyāḍ says:

> This was probably the most complicated issue for the *mutakallimūn* until the *faqīh* 'Abd al Ḥaqq asked Imām Abū al Ma'ālī about it. The latter refused to decide, asserting that to accommodate a *kāfir* in the fold of Islam or to expell a Muslim from it is a very serious religious matter. 'Iyād added that the *qāḍī* Abū Bakr al Bāqillānī has also refused to decide, saying that: 'The people (the Khawārij) did not profess *kufr* but have uttered things which can lead to *kufr*.'

Al Ghazālī says in *al Tafriqah bayn al Īmān wa al Zandiqah*:

> One has to be extremely cautious about branding people *kuffār*. To leave a thousand *kuffār* alive is less serious a wrong than to shed the blood of one Muslim.

Ibn Baṭṭāl says:

> The majority of *'ulamā'* believe that the Khawārij do not stand outside the fold of Islam. 'Alī was asked whether the people of Nahrawān (who were Khawārij) were *kuffār*. He replied: 'They have escaped *kufr*." Ibn Baṭṭāl is also of the opinion that the Khawārij are to be considered *bughāt* if they dissent and initiate war.

The *'ulamā'* have agreed that the issue of *takfir* [to brand people or individuals *kuffār*] is a dangerous one with grave consequences.

2. Duties of Young Muslims

The first duty of the Muslim youth is to rectify their views and thoughts with a view to knowing their *dīn* on the basis of clear evidence and understanding and according to a proper methodology. The right start is acquiring the proper methodology of comprehending Islam, and of dealing with themselves, people and life.

Historically, Muslim scholars have established certain principles and methods which have enhanced the proper comprehension, and deduction of matters and issues whether supported by texts or not. This led to the establishment of the science of *uṣūl al fiqh*: a discipline which studies the methodology of deriving laws from the sources of Islam and of establishing their juristic or constitutional validity. Thus, they established the principles of the controlling and controlled evidence, the subject and object of controlling aspects of evidence: the main and the subsidiary, the imperative and the negative, the general and the particular, the absolute and the restricted, the pronounced and the comprehend. They also established the total aims of the Sharī'ah, such as safeguarding people's welfare, counteracting evil and harm; they divided needs into: essential, necessary and comforts. This is indeed a unique science of which there is no equal, and of which Muslims have the right to be proud. In addition, there are other principles and rules of *fiqh* which may not be available in the books of *uṣūl* but are found in various books on *uṣūl al tafsīr* and Qur'ānic sciences, as well as *uṣūl al ḥadīth*, and Hadith sciences. In addition to these, there are various rules and principles scattered in books of beliefs, hadīth interpretation, and jurisprudence which can be observed by those who have acquired an insight into the purpose of Sharī'ah and its innermost recesses.

What is required, therefore, is not a shallow understanding of the texts but rather a deep knowledge and a genuine comprehension of the purposes of Qur'ānic verses and the *aḥādīth*. The *fiqh*, the awareness, and the knowledge required must take the following into consideration:

First: Knowledge of and insight into Sharī'ah cannot be complete without considering all the particular aspects in relation to the general context of the entire truth of Islam. To issue a judgement a Qur'ānic verse or a ḥadīth must be interpreted in the light of other *aḥādīth*, the *Sunnah* of the Prophet (ṢA'AS) as well as the practice of the companions (RA'A), and must be understood in the light of the Qur'an and the general context and purposes of Sharī'ah. Otherwise there will be a defect in this understanding, and a confusion in deduction and derivation which could create contradictions in Sharī'ah and subject it to ridicule and to calumniations.

For this reason, Imām al Shāṭibī set two conditions for ijtihād: (1) understanding the purposes of Sharī'ah in its totality, and (2) the ability to derive and to draw conclusions on the basis of this understanding.[4] This can only be fulfilled when there is a deep and wide knowledge of the texts, especially the *aḥādīth* and the traditions, in addition to an insight into the reasons, the events, the circumstances, and the purposes of each text, as well as an ability to distinguish between the eternal and unalterable and those formulated to meet a temporary need, an existing custom or tradition, or certain transient circumstances which can be changed when the latter change.[5]

One day I was lecturing on proper Islamic dress for women, according to the Qur'ān and *Sunnah,* when a person in the audience said that the *ḥijāb* mentioned in the Qur'ān must include an additional outer covering. I replied that the *ḥijāb* is not an end in itself, but rather a means for decently covering those parts of the body which the Sharī'ah prohibits to be exposed. In this sense, it can differ from one place and time to another. But the man shouted furiously that the garment required is very clearly specified in a Qur'ānic text, and we therefore have no right to change it. He cited the following verse:

> O Prophet! Tell your wives and daughters and the believing women, that they should cast their outer garments over their persons (when abroad). That is most convenient, that they should be known (as such) and not molested (33:59).

I replied that the Qur'ān sometimes specifies certain means and methods that were suitable and common at the time of the revelation, but were never meant to become permanently binding if better or similar ones are found. The following example is sufficient enough to demonstrate my point. Allah (SWT) said:

> Against them make ready your strength to the utmost of your power, including steeds of war, to strike terror into (the hearts of) the enemies of Allah and your enemies (8:60).

The steed is specifically mentioned above because it was—at the time of revelation—one of the most powerful means known at the time. But there is indeed no reason why Muslims in our times and in earlier days should not use tanks and armored vehicles to achieve the end referred to in the above verse, i.e., to strike fear into the hearts of the enemies of Allah (SWT) and of the enemies of Muslims. Similarly, the woman's outer garment could be any dress which satisfies the objective expressed in verse (33:59) that Muslim women should be recognized and not molested.

---

[4] See *al Muwāfaqāt*, 4:105-106.

[5] See al Qaraḍāwī, Y. *Sharī'at al Islām*.

If such is the case of the Qur'ān, which has an eternal and comprehensive nature, it is only logical that the *Sunnah* is even more open to such an examination. The *Sunnah* comprise a multitude of teachings, the legislative and the nonlegislative, the general and the specific, the eternal and the changeable: a change necessitated by a change in the reasons and the exigencies. In issues and matters related to eating, drinking, and dressing, for example, there are legislative as well as nonlegislative *Sunnah*. Eating with the fingers rather than with silverware is not compulsory. The former method was more natural and suitable to the simple life and nature of the Arabs at the time of the Prophet (ṢA'AS). However this does not mean that using a spoon is *haram* (unlawful) or *makruh* (condemned or discouraged), since it is now so widely available that it in no way indicates any extravagance or excess. But this does not apply to silver or gold tableware, the use of which has clearly been forbidden. Similarly we have to abide by the injunction to eat with the right hand as the purpose of this teaching is fundamental and unalterable, and because it seeks to establish a uniform custom among Muslims, directing them to follow a right-hand approach in everything. The Prophet (ṢA'AS) ordered us: "Say *bism Allah* [before you begin] and eat with your right hand."[6] In another hadith he said: "None of you should eat or drink with his left hand, because Satan eats and drinks with his left hand."[7] Furthermore, during the Prophet's time, Muslims had no idea whatsoever of sieves, which were later known and used to advantage. Could this be regarded as a prohibited innovation or a hateful practice? Of course not.

Another example is the issue of wearing a short *thawb* (garment), which pious young Muslims adhere to and insist on wearing despite the problems which it creates for them, as if it was one of the fundamentals of Islam. These young people put forth two arguments: (1) The dress has to be a short *thawb* because this is the type of dress the Prophet (ṢA'AS) and his companions (RA'A) used. They further believe that other costumes lead us to imitate the *kuffār*, a practice prohibited in Islam; and (2) It has to be short because there are *aḥādīth* which prohibit wearing below-the-ankle *izār* or *thawb* such as: "The part of an *izār* which hangs below the ankles is in the Fire."[8] With regard to the first argument, the Prophet's Sunnah known to us is that he wore whatever was available

---

[6] Agreed upon.

[7] Reported by Muslim.

[8] Reported by al Bukhārī.

to him. For this reason, he wore shirts, robes, and *izārs*. The Prophet (ṢAAS) also wore garments and garbs made in the Yemen and Persia, which were embroidered on the sides with silk. He also wore *'imāmah* (cap) with or without a turban. Al Imām Ibn al Qayyim says in *Al Hady al Nabawī:*

> The best guidance is the *Sunnah* of the Prophet (ṢAAS), the things he regularly practised, ordered, and encouraged people to do. His *sunnah* in dressing is that he used to wear whatever was available for him whether made of cotton, wool, or linen. He is known to have worn cloaks from the Yemen, green cloaks, *jubbah*, garments with full-length sleeves, shirts, pants and robes, shoes and slippers. . . He used, sometimes, to grow a plait in the back.[9]

The textile industry was unknown then, so people used to wear clothes imported from the Yemen, Egypt, and Syria. In our time, we wear—without any inhibition—underwear, headcoverings, shoes, etc., which were unknown during the Prophet's time. Why then this excessive fuss about the *thawb* in particular?

As for the argument of imitating the *kuffār*, we are actually prohibited from imitating their distinguishing characteristics—as followers of other religions—such as sporting the cross, wearing ecclesiastical costumes, celebrating non-Muslim festivals, all of which indicate adherence to a different religion. Ibn Taimīyah explained all this in detail in his book: *Iqtiḍā' al Ṣirāṭ al Mustaqīm fī Mukhālafāt Ahl al Jaḥīm*. With the exception of such conspicuous matters, judgment is made on the basis of intention and purpose. If a Muslim deliberately imitates the *kuffār*, he would be held blameworthy on the basis of his intention. But if a person unintentionally does things which the *kuffār* do, or chooses something which is easier for him, or for his job such as wearing the "overalls" by a factory worker or an engineer, he is not to be held blameworthy. Nonetheless, it is more becoming of a Muslim to distinguish himself from non-Muslims in all material and spiritual matters to the best of his ability. The gist of the matter is that wearing a short *thawb* is more desirable, but wearing a long one is not prohibited if it is just a habit and is not meant to show arrogance, as has already been pointed out.

All the examples given above pertain to purely personal behavior. In that capacity they are less serious than the issues related to the com-

---

[9] See *Zād al Ma'ād*, 1:143.

munity as a whole, the affairs of the state, and international relations which are more complex and constitute a danger to the community, the state, and humanity at large in the absence of an insightful jurisprudence which takes into consideration the proper dimensions of human needs and social interests.

When we call for the resumption of a true Islamic lifestyle and the establishment of a truly Islamic society led by an Islamic state, we must recognize the fact that we live in a world in which human relations are interrelated and complex, ideologies are numerous, distances are shrinking, and barriers are beginning to collapse. It is a world that has become smaller than ever before due to unprecedented technological progress. We must also take into consideration the fact that the community includes the powerful and the weak, men and women, adults and children, the righteous and the transgressor. This diversity must be taken into consideration when we seek to guide, legislate, or give *fatīawā*.

A Muslim who seeks Allah's pleasure may choose to place restrictions on himself and stick to the most extreme and cautious opinions in his endeavor. He can deprive himself of all the means of entertainment such as singing, music, photography, television, etc. But can any modern state afford to do without these? Can any effective journalism do without photography? Can any ministry of Interior—or passport office, immigration or traffic department—or an educational institution do without photography which has become the most important means of discovering and preventing crimes and forgery? Can any contemporary state ignore the times it exists in and deprive its subjects of the invaluable services of television and rely only on the radio, on the grounds that television depends upon photography which is *ḥarām* as some students of "religious education" argue these days?

In short, what I wish to emphasize here is that a person's restrictions on himself may be tolerated and accepted, but it would be intolerable and indeed unacceptable to force these restrictions upon the various groups in the community as a whole. The Prophet said: "Whoever leads people in *ṣalāh* should shorten it because among them are the weak, the old, and those who have business to attend to."[10] This guidance on leading people in *ṣalāh* is also applicable to leading people in any aspect of life.

One of the most serious problems is the failure of some religious people to take account the fact that the *aḥkām* of Sharī'ah are not equally impor-

---

[10] Reported by al Bukhārī.

tant or permanent, and therefore different interpretations can be permitted. There are hypothetical judgments which mainly deal with transactions, customs, and manners. These are open to ijtihād. Disagreement—based on authentic ijtihād—on these issues represents no harm or threat. On the contrary, it is a blessing on the Ummah, and demonstrates flexibility in Sharī'ah and a spaciousness in *fiqh*. There were indeed differences of opinion and disagreement among the Prophet's companions (RA'A)—as well as their successors—on various issues. But such disagreement never caused or created ill-feelings or disunity among them.

On the other hand, there are *aḥkām* dealing with matters of faith, belief, and *'ibādah* which are firmly established in the Qur'ān and *Sunnah* and *ijma'* (consesus), and which have become definitive and categorical. Although they are not requirements of *dīn*, they represent the intellectual and behavioral unity of the Ummah. Deviation from these *ahkam* is a deviation from *Sunnah:* it is sinfulness, prohibited *bid'a* (innovation), and could lead to *kufr*. In addition, there are those *aḥkām* which must be necessarily known and obvious to all people, learned or otherwise. Rejection of these *ahkam* is a clear denial of Allah (SWT) and of His Prophet (ṢA'AS). There should be differention between *aḥkām* based on fundamental or subsidiary issues, whether proven textually or by ijtihād; there should also be differentiation between the categorial and the hypothetical *ahkam* in texts, and between the necessary and the unecessary *ahkam* in *dīn*. Each has its status.

Our great *fuqahā'* have differed widely in their interpretation of some issues, and one can indeed find various opinions on a single issue. There is disagreement, for example, on the heinous sin of murdering a Muslim under duress. Should the punishment fall upon the murderer or upon one who compelled him to do it? Or should it fall upon both or neither, since the crime was not completely premeditated and committed by a single person? All these possibilities were voiced and supported by some *fuqahā'*. Even within each *madhhab* we find different opinions, narrations, ways, and approaches among the *'ulamā'*. Suffice it to say that the subject of that disagreement within Imām Aḥmad's *madhhab*—which is established on and follows tradition—has included enough opinions and narration to fill a twelve-volume book, *al Inṣāf fi al Rājiḥ min al Khilāf.*

In view of this, young Muslims should be fully aware of the issues which are open to disagreement and those which are not. But more importantly, they should know the standard norms of behavior practised in settling differences and disagreements. They must learn *adab al khilāf* (ethics of disagreement),[11] which we have inherited from our *a'immah* and *'ulamā'.* We must learn from them how to be open-minded and tolerant toward those with whom we disagree about subsidiary religious matters. How can we differ and disagree yet remain united brothers who love and respect each other and who refrain from exchanging accusations? First of all, we must realize that disagreements on marginal and subsidiary matters and issues are natural. There is indeed a Divine wisdom in making a few *aḥkām* in Sharī'ah categorical in both their definitiveness and meaning, and in making hypothetical ones which constitute the bulk of *aḥkām* and on which there is broad scope for fruitful disagreement.

It is a blessing that Allah (SWT) has bestowed on some Muslim *'ulamā'* the ability to ascertain, to examine closely, and to decide on matters of disagreement without prejudice against any *madhhab* or opinion. These include the following *a'immah*: Ibn Daqīq al 'Īd, Ibn Taymīyah, Ibn Qayyim, Ibn Kathīr, Ibn Ḥajar al 'Asqalānī, al Dahlawī, al Shawkānī, al Ṣan'ānī, and others. But differences are bound to arise and continue because they are deeply rooted in the nature of man, life, language and – Divine commandment. Attempts to eradicate these differences will fail, because they will actually be battling against human nature, against life, against all *sunan*. As we have already mentioned, disagreement based on authentic ijtihād which does not create discord or disunity is a blessing for the Ummah and an enrichment of *fiqh*. Objective disagreement in itself poses no threat if it is coupled with tolerance and open-mindedness, and if it is free from fanaticism, accusations, and narrow-mindedness. The Prophet's Companions differed among themselves on many issues and practical *aḥkām,* but they still never condemned one another and had very cordial and strong relations. 'Umar ibn 'Abd al 'Azīz said: "I never wished that the Prophet's companions had not had disagreements. Their disagreement was a mercy."

Different interpretations even emerged during the life of the Prophet (ṢA'AS). These were sanctioned by him, and he did not single out one party or group for blame. Immediately after the battle of the Aḥzāb, the Prophet (ṢA'AS) said to his Companions: "Whoever believes in Allah and the Last Day must not perform *ṣalāt al 'aṣr* until he has reached [the dwellings of] Banū Qurayẓah."[12] Some of the Companions found

---

[11] See Ṭāhā Jābir al 'Alwānī, *Adab al Ikhtilāf fī al Islām,* 1987. The first edition was published in *Kitāb al Ummah* series in Qatar. Two reprints were published by the International Institute of Islamic Thought, Herndon, VA, USA. The publication of the French and English versions is underway. [Editors' note].

[12] Reported by al Bukhārī and Muslim.

this practically impossible, and therefore performed *ṣalāt al 'Aṣr* before reaching their destination. Others—who were literalists—only performed *ṣalāh* when they reached the dwellings of Banū Qurayẓah as the Prophet (ṢA'AS) had asked them. When the Prophet (ṢA'AS) was told, he approved of the action of both parties although one of them must have been wrong.

This clearly indicates that there is no sin in acting upon an interpretation which is based on solid evidence, sincere genuine intention and ijtihād. Ibn al Qayyim described those who applied the essence of *aḥādīth* as *Ahl al Qiyās* (analogy applicants) and those who applied the letter of *aḥādīth* as Ẓahirī'yah (literalists).

Unfortunately, there are people these days who not only assume that they know the whole truth and all the answers, but who also try to coerce other people to follow them, believing that they can eradicate all *madhāhib* and disagreements and unite all people in one single stroke. They tend to forget that their own understanding and interpretation of the texts are no more than hypotheses which may be right or wrong. Moreover, no human (i.e., no *'ālim*) is infallible, even though he may satisfy all the conditions and requisities of ijtihād. All that is certain is the reward he will obtain for his ijtihād, whether it was right or wrong, should the intention be sincere. Therefore, such people would achieve nothing except the creation of an additional *madhhab*! It is strange and absurd that while they disapprove of people's adherence to different *madhāhib*, they themselves try to persuade people to imitate them and follow their new *madhhab*.

No one should jump to the conclusion that I reject their call for adherence to the texts or their own interpretations and understanding. This is absolutely the right granted to everyone who can fulfill the conditions of ijtihād and its means. No one has the right to close the gates of ijtihād which were opened by the Prophet (ṢA'AS) for the whole Ummah. What I do reject is their self-presumption, arrogance, vanity, and disregard for the findings of their learned predecessors, their disrespect for the *fiqh* we have inherited from our great forebears. I reject their false claim that they alone are right, as well as their erroneous impression that they can eliminate disparity and disagreement and unite people on one opinion—their own.

One of the followers of this "one-opinion" school asked me once why all Muslims should not agree on the juristic opinion supported by the text. I replied that the text first has to be authentic and accepted by all, its meaning has to be plain, and it should not be contradicted by another text, whether stonger or similar in evidence. There should be full agreement as regards the three preceding points. A text may be regarded as authentic by an *imām*, but another *imām* may see it as weak or as authentic but without proven evidence justifying its given meaning; a text may be regarded as general by an *imām* but as particular by another, or it may be seen as absolute or restricted; it may also be regarded as categorical or abrogated. Such variance leads to producing different *aḥkām*, i.e. something may be *wājib* or *ḥarām*, *mustaḥabb* or *makrūh*. In short, all these difference fall within the considerations pointed out by Ibn Taymīyah in his book, *Raf' al Malām 'an al A'immat al A'lām*, and mentioned by Walīy Allāh al Dahlawī in his book, *Ḥujjat Allah al Bālighah*, and in his, *al Inṣāf fī Asbāb al Ikhtilāf*, and detailed by al Shaykh 'Alī al Khafīf in his book, *Asbāb Ikhtilāf al Fuqahā'.*

Let us consider the following *aḥādīth*:

1. "Any woman who wears a gold necklace will be made to wear a similar one [made] of fire on the Day of Judgment. And any woman who wears gold earrings will have a similar one [made of fire] on the Day of Judgment."[13]

2. "Whoever desires his beloved to wear a ring [made] of fire [on the Day of Judgment], let him give him [her] [to wear] a gold ring. And whoever desires his beloved to wear a necklace [made] of fire [on the Day of Judgment], let him give him [her] [to wear] a gold necklace. And whoever desires his beloved to wear a bracelet [made] of fire [on the Day of Judgment], let him give him [her] [to wear] a gold bracelet. But you can do whatever you please with silver."[14]

3. It is also related by Thawbān (RA'A) that the Prophet (ṢA'AS) warned his daughter Fāṭimah (RA'A) against wearing a gold chain. In response, she sold it, bought a slave with the money, and set him free. When the Prophet (ṢA'AS) was told of this, he said: "Thanks to Allah (SWT) who rescued Fāṭimah from the Fire."[15]

Justists have different attitudes toward these *aḥādīth:*

1. Some have examined their *isnād*[16] and, finding them weak, rejected

[13] Reported by Abū Dāwūd and al Nasā'ī.

[14] Reported by Abū Dāwūd.

[15] Reported by al Nasā'ī.

[16] Ascription, *Al Musnad*: "Any collection of *aḥādīth* in which the *aḥādīth* are arranged according to the chain of reporters who related them.

them and considered them insufficiant for prohibition, which requires clear-cut evidence and careful investigation, especially with respect to matters of general concern and which Muslims have generally accepted.

2. Others have agreed that the *isnād* is correct but that the *aḥādīth* have been revoked because other evidence in other sources have permitted women to adorn themselves with gold. Al Bayhaqī and others have reported the consensus on this matter which has been accepted in *fiqh* and become a standard practice.

3. Some considered the *ahadith* applicable to those who have not given *zakah* on the gold they have, basing their opinion on other *ahadith* which have not, themselves, escaped criticism. Furthermore. *zakah* on women's jewellery is a subject of disagreement among the different *madhahib.*

4. Some jusrists argue that these *aḥādīth* seek to warn women who vainly adorn themselves with gold, deliberately intending to draw attention to their wealth. Al Nasā'ī also reported some *aḥādīth* which are relevant to this issue under the title: *Bāb al Karāhīyah li al Nisā' fi Iẓhār Ḥilī al Dhahab* (Disapproval of Women's Display of Golden Jewelry). Other jurists say that they arc related only to excessive adornment out of vanity or pride.

5. In our own times, Shaykh Nāṣir al Dīn al Albānī has come out with an opinion different from the consensus on permitting women to adorn themselves with gold, which has been accepted by all *madhāhib* for the last fourteen centuries. He not only believes that the *isnād* of these *aḥādīth* is authentic, but that these texts are categorical in this matter; i.e. prohibiting gold rings and earrings. In this he disagreed with the consensus of the *fiqh* of all *madhāhib* and the practice of the Ummah throughout the past fourteen hundred years.

Has the existence of these *aḥādīth* prevented disagreement on their authenticity or guidance? Can the modern "traditionalist school" eradicate disagreement and unite all people on one opinion on the basis of a ḥadīth or a tradition which they use as evidence? The answer is clear enough: people will continue to disagree and differ amongst themselves, and this will, *in shā'a Allāh,* pose no danger or problem. Allah *ta'ālā* says: "To each is a goal to which Allah turns him" (2:148).

In this respect, I feel inclined to admit that the religious leader who, in this age, has understood the essence and ethics of disagreements was Ḥasan al Bannā (d. 1949). He brought up his followers to believe in and adhere to these ethics. Despite his unflinching commitment to the cause of Muslim solidarity and his sincere efforts to unite the various Muslim groups and make them agree at least on mimimum Islamic concepts and principals, as is clear from his own known work *al Uṣūl al 'Ishrūn,* he was convinced of the inevitability of disagreement on the subsidiary issues and the practical *aḥkām* of Islam. This he has eloquently discussed in many of his messages which have proved to be useful. In *Da'watuna* (Our Da'wah), al Bannā spoke of the characteristics of his *da'wah* as being general ones which neither patronize a particular sect nor advocate a particular line of thought. Interest is in the core of *dīn* and its essence; it hopes that all endeavors are united so that a more fruitful work can be done to produce greater results; it supports truth everywhere; it likes consensus and dislikes eccentricity; it attributes a great deal of the mishaps which have befallen Muslims to misguided disagreement and to disunity; it believes that love and unity are the major factor of their victories, and that the only hope for invigorating and revitalizing the present-day Ummah lies in reviving and adopting the practice of the early generations of Muslims. But, in spite of his strong belief in the necessity of unity and dislike of disunity, al Bannā wrote:

> We believe that disagreements on subsidiary religious issues are inevitable for various reasons, the most important of which are:
>
> Intellectual differences resulting from the level of intelligence and depth of knowledge, the multiplicity and interrelatedness of the facts, and the inherent ambiguities of the Arabic language which are bound to affect the interpretation of the texts. In all these people are different, and therefore disagreement is inevitable.
>
> The abundance of the sources of knowledge in some parts of the Islamic world and their scarcity in other places is also an important factor. Mālik said to Abū Ja'far: "The Prophet's companions scattered into remote regions, each group possessing specific knowledge. If you were to force them to follow one opinion you would create *fitnah*.[17]
>
> There are also cultural differences. Al Shāfi'ī (RA'A) used to give different *fatāwā* in accordance with the different conditions prevailing in Iraq and in Egypt. In both cases he used to base his verdict upon what he believed to be truth.

---

[17] "Misguidance, dissuasion from one's Islamic commitment."

The opinion of the imām toward the narrator is another factor. One imām may consider a narrator fully reliable, but another may have doubts about the same narrator and consequently refrain from taking what he has transmitted in full confidence.

Also, a cause of difference lies in assessing the evidence of *aḥkām;* some give precedence to people's practices over *aḥādīth* narrated through by one single narrator, etc.

For these reasons we believe that a consensus on subsidiary religious matters is not only impossible but incompatible with the nature of *dīn,* because such a demand is bound to generate rigidity and excessiveness, which are contrary to the Islamic imperatives of flexibility, facilitation, and simplicity. Doubtless, these virtues will enable Islam to meet the requirements of all times.

Furthermore, we understand the reasons of those who disagree with us on subsidiary and marginal issues. Such disagreement does not affect our mutual love or cooperation, as we are all contained within the comprehensiveness of Islam. Aren't we all Muslim, required to like for our Muslim brothers what we like for ourselves? Why disagreement then, and why cannot each of us have our different opinions, and also try to reach an agreement, if possible, in an atmosphere of candor and love?

The companions of the Prophet (ṢA'AS) had disagreed in *fatwā,* but that did not create any disunity or rupture. The incident of the *ṣalāh* and Banū Qurayẓah is a case in point. If these who have known the *aḥkām* better than us have had their disagreements, isn't it absurd that we maliciously disagree with each other on frivolous matters? If our *a'immah,* who more than any one else know the Qur'ān and *Sunnah,* have had their disagreements and their debates, why cannot we do the same? If there was disagreement on even clear and well-known subsidiary issues, such as the five-times-a-day *adhān,* which were supported by texts and by tradition, what about the more delicate issues which are subject to opinion and deduction?

We also need to remember that during the time of the Caliphate, disagreements were referred to, and settled by, the

Caliph. Since there are no caliphs these days, Muslims must find a judge to which they can refer their case. Otherwise, their disagreement will lead to another disagreement.

Finally, our brothers are fully aware of all this and have consequently more patience and open-mindedness. They believe that each group of people has specific knowledge and that in each *da'wah* there are elements of truth as well as falsity. They carefully investigate the truth and accept it, and they try with amicability to convince those who are wrong. If the latter are convinced it is indeed very good, but if they are not they remain our Muslim brothers. We ask Allah to guide us and to guide them.*

The above is a brief summary of Imām al Bannā's views on juristic disagreements and his attitude toward them. It clearly shows his deep knowledge of Islam, of history, and of reality.

I would also like to relate an ancident in al Bannā's life—which could have been the experience of other *'ulamā'* as well—to illustrate these concepts and views. One day during Ramaḍān, al Banna was invited to deliver a lecture in a small village in Egypt. The people in that village were divided into two groups which held different opinions regarding the number of *raka'āt* in *ṣalāt al tarāwīḥ.* One group argued that according to the tradition of 'Umar ibn al Khaṭṭāb (RA'A), they should be twenty. The other group insisted that they must be eight, maintaining that it was known that the Prophet (ṢA'AS) never exceeded this number at any time. Accordingly, each group accused the other of *bid'ah,* and their disagreement reached a dangerous level, almost leading to open physical conflict. When al Bannā arrived they agreed to refer the matter to him.

The way he handled this event is instructive to all of us. He first asked: "What is the juristic status of *ṣalāt al tarāwīḥ*?" The answer was: "A *sunnah,* and those who perform it are rewarded, those who do not are not punished." He then asked: "And what is the juristic status of brotherhood among Muslims?" The people replied: "*farḍ* [Obligatory], and it is one of the fundamentals of *īmān.*" He then concluded: "Is it therefore logical or permissible according to Sharī'ah to abandon a *farḍ* for a *sunnah?*" He then told them that if they preserved their brotherhood and unity and each went home and performed *ṣalāt al tarāwīḥ* according to his own genuine conviction, it would indeed be far better then arguing and quarreling.

* Al Bannā, Ḥasan; *Da'watunā*

When I mentioned this to some people, they said that al Bannā's action was evasive—an escape from the truth, i.e., from pointing out the difference between a *sunnah and a bid'ah.* This, they insisted, is the duty of a Muslim. I replied that this is a matter where there is room for different opinions, and that although I perform eight *raka'āt,* I do not accuse those performing twenty of *bid'ah.* They persisted that making a decision on such matters is a duty which a Muslim must not evade. I insisted that this is true when the choice is between *ḥalāl* and *ḥarām,* but in matters on which the juristic schools of thought have had their disagreements and, consequently, each one of us his own view, there is no need for bigotry or zealotry.

Many fair Muslim *'ulamā'* have clearly sanctioned this. The following quotation is from one of the *Ḥanābilah* books entitled *Sharḥ Ghāyat al Muntahā:*

> Whoever rejects an opinion reached by ijtihād does so because of his ignorance of the status of the *mujtahidūn* who will be rewarded, be they right or wrong, for their laborious, time-consuming findings in this respect. Those who follow them commit no sin, because Allah has ordained for each of them that to which his ijtihād had led him, and which becomes part of the Sharī'ah in that respect. There is an example in the permission to eat, out of dire necessity only, the meat of a dead animal. However, this is prohibited for a person who deliberately chooses to do so. Both of these are well-established juristic verdicts.

Ibn Taymīyah says in *al Fatāwā al Miṣrīyah:*

> Consideration of unity [among Muslims] is the right course. The *basmalah* can be uttered loudly to fulfill a commendable interest. It is also advisable to abandon the preferable in order to create harmony and intimacy, just as the Prophet (ṢA'AS) gave up the re-building of the Ka'bah [on the foundations laid down by Ibrāhīm] so as not to alienate [the people of Makkah]. The *a'immah,* like Imām Aḥmad, are of this opinion with regard to the *basmalah,* to replace the preferable with the acceptable in order to preserve unity.

Ibn Taymīyah referred to the following ḥadīth with regard to the building of the Ka'bah. The Prophet (SA'AS) said to 'Ā'ishah (RA'A): "Had your people not been in *jāhilīyah* (the attitudes and mentality of pre-Islamic time) until recently, I would have rebuilt the Ka'bah on the foundations [laid] by Ibrāhīm."

Ibn al Qayyim also discussed the issue of *qunūt*[17] in *ṣalāt al fajr.* Some people have considered *qunūt* as *bid'ah,* others as supererogatory to be practised in times of hardships as well as other times. In his book *Zād al Ma'ād,* he argues that the Prophet's *Sunnah* sanctions *qunūt* during the times of hardship, and that this has been accepted by ḥadīth scholars who follow what the Prophet (ṢA'AS) did. They therefore did *qunūt* at the times the Prophet (ṢA'AS) is known to have done *qunūt* and abstained from it at the times he is known to have abstained from *qunūt.* They see *qunūt* as a *sunnah* and abstaining from it as also a *sunnah.* Therefore they neither object to those who continually do *qunūt* or to those who abstain from it, and they do not consider it *bid'ah.* Ibn al Qayyim writes:

> A proper posture to ask Allah's blessings and to offer thanks to Him is when a person stands up after kneeling in *ṣalāh.* The Prophet (SẠ'AS) did both in this posture. It is acceptable for the imām to utter *qunūt* prayers these loudly so that the people behind him can hear. 'Umar ibn al Khaṭṭāb raised his voice when reciting the *Fātiḥah,* and so did Ibn 'Abbās during the *ṣalāh* for the dead in order to let people know that it is sunnah to do so. Such practices are subject to acceptable disagreement; neither those who do them nor those who refrain are blameworthy: the same applies to raising the hands during *ṣalāh,* the various ways of *tashahhud, adhān, iqāmah,* as well as the types of *ḥajj* as *ifrād, qirān* and *tamattu'.*
>
> Our purpose is only to mention the Prophet's *Sunnah,* which is our guiding principle in this book and which we seek to investigate. Having said that, I wish to point out that I have not tried to deal with what is permissible and what is not. Our concern is with the permissible practice which the Prophet (ṢA'AS) used to choose for himself, and which is the best and most perfect. If we say that there is no indication in his *Sunnah* that he consistently performed *qunūt* during *ṣalāt al Fajr* or uttered the *basmalah* loudly, this does not mean or indicate that we should consider consistency in performing them as *makrūh* or *bid'ah.* It only means that his guidance is the best and most perfect.[18]

[18] *Zād al Ma'ād,* 1:144.

Moreover, an individual is permitted to continue his *ṣalāh* behind an imām of a different *madhhab* even if he believes that the latter has done something which nullifies his ablution, or makes his *ṣalāh* nugatory, if the imām's *madhhab* permits that. Ibn Taymīyah says in *al Fawākih al 'Adīdah:*

> Muslims are unanimous on the admissibility of performing *ṣalāh* behind each other as was the practice of the Companions and the *Tābi'ūn,* as well as that of the four great jurists of Islam. Whoever rejects this practice is a straying *mubtadi'* who deviates from the teaching of the Qur'ān, *Sunnah,* and the consensus of the Muslims.
>
> Although some of the companions and the *Tābi'ūn* uttered the *basmalah* loudly and other did not, they nevertheless continued to perform *ṣalāh* behind each other. So did Abū Ḥanīfah and his followers, as well as al Shāfi'ī and others who used to perform *ṣalāh* behind the *Mālikīyah* in Madīnah, although the latter did not utter the *basmalah,* neither loudly nor in their hearts. It is said that Abū Yūsuf performed *ṣalāh* behind al Rashīd who had been cupped.[19] Because al Imām Mālik has given a *fatwā* that there is no need to renew ablutions in this case, Abū Yūsuf continued his *ṣalāh* behind al Rashīd.
>
> However, Aḥmad ibn Ḥanbal was of the opinion that ablution must be done after cupping and nosebleeding. Confronted with a hypothetical situation whether a member of the congregation who notices a discharge of blood from the imām, who does not renew his ablution, should continue his *ṣalāh* behind him, Ibn Ḥanbal said: "It is inconceivable not to perform *ṣalāh* behind Sa'īd ibn al Musayyab and Mālik." He then added that there are two considerations in this issue: (1) If the man is not aware of anything that invalidates the imām's *ṣalāh* he should continue behind him. This is agreed upon by the forebears and the four great jurists; and (2) If he was sure that the *imām* has done something which renders him impure, such as touching his genitals or women out of sexual desire, cupping or vomiting, and did not renew his ablu-

[19] Cupping is an operation of drawing blood to the surface of the body by use of a glass vessel evacuated by heat (a form of treatment). It is generally considered as one of the things which nullify ablution.

tion, he then must act according to his best judgement, because this is an issue about which there is a great deal of disagreement. The majority of our forebears are of the opinion that the *ṣalāh* of those behind such an imām is valid. This is the opinion of Mālik's *madhhab,* but a second opinion in al Shāfi'ī's and Abū Ḥanīfah's. Most of Aḥmad's texts support this opinion, which is the correct one.[20]

3. Knowledge, Values, and Actions

Knowledge of, and *fiqh* in, *dīn* help in the assessment of the value as well as the status, in the *Sharī'ah,* of actions and duties which have their specific place in the scale of the commandments and the prohibitions. Such knowledge prevents any confusion regarding status, variations, or similarities concerning the juristic value of actions. Islam has given a specific value to each specific action according to its positive influence on life or according to the degree of damage and negative effect which it may create.

Among the **commandments** there is the *mustaḥabb,* (the commendable) action, the neglect of which is not punishable but the performance of which is rewardable. There is also the confirmed *Sunnah* of the Prophet (ṢA'AS) such as things which he always did, never neglected, but did not categorically command others to do. The companions (RA'A) used to neglect some of these to prove that they were not *wājib.* For this reason, both Abū Bakr and 'Umar used to refrain from offering *dhabiḥah* (animal sacrifice). Another type of *wājib* according to some *madhāhib,* is that which is commanded but not categorically ordained. *Farḍ* is that which is categorically and unequivocally obligatory and whose performance is rewarded and negligence punished; failure to observe it is *fisq,* sinfulness, or iniquity; failure to believe in it is *kufr.*

It is common knowledge that *farḍ* is classified into two categories: *farḍ kifāyah* (collective obligation), and *farḍ 'ayn* (individual obligation). The individual obligation has to be performed by each Muslim. The collective obligation, on the other hand, entails no punishment on those who have not participated in it if others have done so. Individual obligations are further classified. The most important are those *farā'iḍ* which

[20] See *Al Fawākih al 'Adīdah,* 2:181. See also al Qaraḍāwī, Y. *Fatāwā Mu'āṣirah,* pp. 201-207, second edition.

are considered in Islam fundamental articles of faith: the *shahādah*—i.e., the act of witnessing that there is no god but Allah and that Muḥammad is His Prophet, Servant, and Messenger, the verbal content of that act—*ṣalāh, zakāh, ṣiyām,* and *ḥajj* for those who can afford the journey. There are other *farā'iḍ* of a lesser status than the aforementioned, but they are still absolutely compulsory. There is no doubt that Islam gives precedence to *farḍ 'ayn* over *farḍ kifāyah.* Thus kindness and submission to parents, which is *farḍ 'ayn* has precedence over *jihād,* as long as it is *farḍ kifāyah.* A son is therefore not allowed to participate in *jihād* without the prior consent and permission of the parents. This is enshrined in authentic *aḥādīth.* Moreover, a *farḍ 'ayn* which is connected with the rights of the community has precedence over another *farḍ 'ayn* which is connected with the rights of an individual, or a number of individuals, like *jihād* and devotion to parents. Therefore in the case of foreign aggression against a Muslim land, *jihād* becomes *farḍ 'ayn* with a precedence over the rights of parents. Further, *farḍ* has precedence over *wājib, wājib* over *sunnah,* and confirmed *sunnah* over *mustaḥabb.* Islam also gives precedence to acts of common social nature over those which concern individual kinship, and prefers acts which benefit more than one person to those which only benefit an individual. For this reason Islam prefers *jihād* and *fiqh* over personal *'ibādah,* reconciliation between warring parties over voluntary *ṣalāh, ṣiyām,* and *ṣadaqah.* Similarly, "a just ruler is rewarded more for his adherence to justice for a single day than he is for his performance of voluntary *'ibādah* for sixty years".

Some of the grave mistakes committed by Muslims during the period of decline and decadence are outlined below:

1. They neglected—to a great extent—the collective duties of concern to the whole Ummah such as scientific, industrial, and military advancement and excellence, without which Muslims cannot attain strength or power. They neglected ijtihād, inference of *aḥkām, da'wah,* and the opposition to unjust rulers.
2. They also neglected some individual *farḍ 'ayn* obligations, or at least underrated their value, such as the obligation on every Muslim to command the common good and to prohibit evil and the undesirable.
3. They gave more attention to some of the fundamental pillars of faith at the expense of others; thus they paid more attention to *ṣiyām* during Ramaḍān than *ṣalāh.* That is why those who offered *ṣiyām* were more than those who performed *ṣalāh,* especially among the women. There were indeed those who never prostrated before Allah (SWT) in prayer.

Moreover, there were those who gave more attention to *ṣalāh* that *zakāh,* although Allah (SWT) combined both in twenty-eight places in the Qur'ān, which made some of the Companions (RA'A) said that "The *ṣalāh* of a person who does not give *zakāh* is invalid." And it is for this reason that Abū Bakr al Siddīq swore to declare war on those who failed to equate between *ṣalāh* with *zakāh.*

4. They attached more importance to some *nawāfil* (supererogulataries) than they did to *furūḍ* or *wājibāt.* This can be observed in the practice of the Sufis, who concentrate on rituals, *dhikr,* and *tasbīḥ* and neglect collective duties such as condemnation of corruption and resistance to social and political injustice.

5. They paid more attention to individual *'ibādah,* such as *ṣalāh* and *dhikr,* and neglected the collective *'ibadah* such as *jihād, fiqh,* reconciliation between people, and cooperation in the dissemination of righteousness, piety, compassion, and tolerance.

6. Finally, most people attached a great deal of importance to subsidiary matters at the expense of fundamental issues such as belief, *īmān,* and *tawhīd* (unization of God), as well as the goal of moral and spiritual efforts, i.e., the seeking of Allah's pleasure.

The **prohibitions** are classified into the following: those which are *makrūhāt* (hateful) but do not entail punishment; those which are detested but not categorically prohibited and are therefore nearer to *ḥarām* than *ḥalāl.* The *mutashābihāt* (doubtful) are those not known to many people and are therefore committed out of ignorance. Those who commit then commit *ḥarām.* The categorical *ḥarām* (unlawful prohibitions) are those detailed in the Qur'ān and *Sunnah.* Allah (SWT) says: "Why should you not eat of [meats] on which Allah's name has been pronounced, when He has explained to you in detail what is forbidden to you?" (6:119).

These prohibitions are divided into two: major and minor. The minor ones can be expiated by the performance of religious devotions such as *ṣalāh, ṣiyām,* and charity. We learn in the Qur'ān that "Good deeds remove those that are evil" (11:114). In the Prophet's traditions we learn that constant adherence to the five daily *ṣalawāt, ṣalat al jumu'ah,* and *ṣiyām,* during Ramaḍān expiates whatever minor sins a person may commit in between if he avoids the major ones. Those can only expiated by genuine repentance. The worst of these sins is *shirk*—the association of other beings with Allah (SWT)—a sin which is never forgiven:

> Allah does not forgive that partners should be set up with Him; but He forgives anything else to whom He pleases; to

> set up partners with Allah is to devise a sin most heinous indeed (4:48).

Next in order are sins mentioned in *aḥādīth* such as: disobedience to parents, bearing false witness, sorcery, murder, usury, taking liberty with the property and money of orphans, and false accusation—especially of fornication—of chaste Muslim women.

Defectiveness and confusion have resulted from the following:

1. People are more busy trying to stem *makrūhāt* or *mutashābihāt* than *muḥarramāt* and the negligence of *wājibāt.* Also, their concern is for those matters on which there is disagreement as to whether they are *ḥalāl* or *ḥarām,* rather than those matters which are categorically *ḥarām.*
2. Many people are too absorbed in trying to resist the minor rather than the major and mortal sins such as fortune-telling, sorcery, consecration, using the tombs of certain people as places of *ṣalāh* and *'ibādah,* making animal sacrifices for dead people, seeking help from the dead and so on. Such sins contaminate the purity of *tawhīd.*

Similarly, people, i.e., individual Muslims, are different. Some religious youth commit a gross mistake when they look at and treat people as if they were similar and equal in their knowledge, endurance, *īmān,* etc., and therefore fail to distinguish between the people at large and the learned and committed Muslim; between those who have only recently embraced Islam and those whose beliefs are well-established; between the weak and the strong; in spite of the fact that there is room in Islam for every one of these according to their status and their readiness. In recognition of these natural differences, Islam provides opportunities for perseverance and facility, *farā'iḍ,* and *nawāfil,* and the obligatory and the voluntary. Hence Allah (SWT) says:

> Then We have given the Book for inheritance to such of Our servants as We have chosen: but there are among them some who wrong their own souls; some who follow a middle course; and some who are by Allah's leave, foremost in good deeds. That is the highest grace (35:32).

In this respect, the person who wrongs himself has been defined as he who commits prohibitions and whose observance of the obligatory duties is incomplete. And the person who follows a middle course is he who performs only the obligatory duties and eschews prohibitions. The person who is foremost in good deeds" is he "who, in addition to performing the obligatory as well as the recommended, eschews not only prohibitions, but also the recommended against as well as the doubtful acts. All these types of people, including the person who wrongs himself, are included in the fold of Islam, and belong to the chosen Islamic Ummah to whom Allah (SWT) has given the Qur'ān: "Then We have given the Book for inheritence to such of Our servants as We have chosen" (35:32). It is therefore wrong and indeed nonsensical to exclude people from the fold of Islam and the Ummah simply because they have wronged themselves. It is equally wrong to fail to recognize and admit such classification and to treat people as if they are all foremost in good deeds. Consequently, enthusiastic young Muslims should not hasten to accuse other Muslims of *fisq,* to show animosity and antipathy toward them simply because they have committed some minor sins or some acts on which judgment is obscure and on which there is contradicting evidence, and which cannot therefore be considered as absolutely *ḥarām.* In their own sincerity to their cause, these young people have forgotten that the Qur'ān has clearly distinguished between minor and major sins or faults: the former do not exclude the Muslim from the fold of Islam and can be expiated by eschewing the latter. Allah (SWT) says:

> Yes, to Allah belongs all that is in the heavens and on earth. He rewards those who do evil according to their deeds, and He rewards those who do good with what is best. Those who avoid great sins and shameful deeds, only [falling into] small faults, verily, your Lord is ample in forgiveness (53:31-32).

The core of the principle for tolerating small faults or sins lies in the interpretation of the Arabic word *lamam* (small faults). There are two important interpretations of *lamam* which we must not overlook. Al *Ḥāfiẓ* Ibn Kathīr says the following is his own interpretation of verses 255-256 in *Sūrat al Nisā':*

> The word *muḥsinūn* has been interpreted to mean those who avoid great sins and shameful deeds, i.e., the major prohibitions. If such people commit small faults, Allah will forgive and protect them, as He promised in another verse: "If you [but] eschew the most heinous of the things which you are forbidden to do, we shall expel out of you all the evil in you, and admit you to a gate of great honor (4:31). "...Those who avoid great sins and shameful deeds only commit small faults," which is a clear exclusion since small faults *lamam* are subcategories of minor sins and shameful acts.

Ibn Kathīr then mentioned the following: Ibn 'Abbās said, "I have not come across things which are closer to *lamam* than in the following ḥadīth narrated by Abū Hurayrah:

> Allah has decreed for Ādam's son [Man] his share of fornication which he will inevitably commit. The fornication of the eye is the gaze [to look at things which a person is forbidden]; the fornication of the tongue is the utterance; the inner self wishes and desires, and the private parts testify to this or deny it.[21]

Hence, Ibn Mas'ūd and Abū Hurayrah say that *lamam* includes gazing, winking, kissing, and approaching sexual intercourse without committing actual fornication.

The other interpretation of *lamam* is also related by Ibn 'Abbās to mean a person who commits a shameful deed but repents of it. He then quoted a line of a verse which can be paraphrased to mean: "Allah, O Your Forgiveness is plenteous, because there is no one among Your servants who does not commit small faults."[22] Abū Hurayrah and al Ḥasan supported the above. Some also argue that *lamam* are those which are committed by a person without seriously giving them consideration, and not very often. All this means is that there is enough room in Islam for everyone who does not persistently commit great sins, because Allah's mercy extends to all those who repent.

One of the most instructive Islamic examples for teaching people how to overlook the small mistakes and faults of those who perform the obligatory duties, as man is not infallible nor an angel, comes from the attitude of 'Umar ibn al Khaṭṭāb (RA'A). It is related[23] that some people went to 'Abd Allah ibn 'Umar when he was in Egypt and told him that they observed that many teachings of the Qur'ān were not being adhered to by their contemporaries, and wanted to question the Caliph, 'Umar ibn al Khaṭṭāb, about this matter. 'Abd Allah then took them to 'Umar (RA'A) in Madīnah. When 'Umar met 'Abd Allah, the latter informed him of the purpose of the visit and of the people who came with him. 'Umar (RA'A) then asked 'Abd Allah to arrange for a meeting. When the people from Egypt came to the meeting, 'Umar (RA'A) turned to the nearest of them and said: "Tell me truly, have you read the whole

---

[21] Reported by Aḥmad, al Bukhārī, and Muslim.

[22] Reported by Ibn Kathīr on the authority of Ibn Jarīr and al Tirmidhī. Al Tirmidhī regards it authentic but odd.

[23] Reported by Ibn Kathīr on the authority of Ibn 'Awn who quotes al Ḥasan al Baṣrī.

Qur'ān?" The man answered in the affirmative. 'Umar then asked him consecutive questions: "Have you yourself strictly followed its teachings in your intentions, in order to purify your heart and to reflect on your actions?" The man answered in the negative. 'Umar (RA'A) then asked: "Have you strictly followed its teaching in your gaze [by not looking at things which Allah has prohibited], in your utterance, and in your living?" To each of these the man answered in the negative. 'Umar (RA'A) then asked the same questions of the other members of the group who all answered in the negative to each question.

'Umar (RA'A) then said: "How can you demand from him [the Caliph, in this instance 'Umar himself] to force people to adhere to your own understanding of Allah's Book when you yourselves have failed to do that as you have admitted? Our Lord knows that each one of us is liable to commit some evil actions." He then recited the following verse: "If you [but] eschew the most heinous of the things which you are forbidden to do, we shall expel out of you all the evil in you and admit you to a gate of great honor" (4:31).

Turning to the group he asked: "Do the people of Madīnah know why you are here?" When they answered in the negative, he then said: "Had they known, I would have made an example of you [by severe punishment]." This incident is narrated by Ibn Jarīr in Ibn Kathīr's *tafsīr,* and 'Uqbah approved its authencity and *isnād.*

With this far-sighted knowledge and insight into the Qur'ān, 'Umar was able to settle this issue immediately on the spot, and therefore prevented an infiltration of bigotry and zealotry. Had he shown any leniency in the matter, a great *fitnah* with far-reaching grave consequences could have been initiated.

4. Sympathetic Understanding of the Abilities, Limitations, and Circumstances of Others

Another aspect of *fiqh* lacking in extremists is to cherish a sympathetic understanding of and a deep appreciation for the varying levels of individual abilities , limitations and circumstances which may hinder other Muslims in coping with the requirements of ideal Islamic life. It would be a great mistake to expect or demand all people to become martyrs like Ḥamzah ibn 'Abd al Muṭṭalib (RA'A) by firmly standing up against the perpetrators of oppression, injustice, and exploitation, and to sacrifice everything for the cause of *da'wah*. This is a virtue which none but the exceptionally persevering few can aspire to or actually realize.

Some people may be content with only quietly voicing the truth; others may even resort to complete silence out of their conviction that the prevailing conditions have reached such a dominance that it is futile, and probably dangerous, to object openly or try to change things. Others may believe that reform must begin from the bottom, not from the top, and thus direct their efforts towards individuals who they believe are capable of effecting the desired change and reform after being armed with clarity of vision and purpose, though the eradication of Westernized and secular regimes and systems cannot be realized without a deep-rooted and long-term collective struggle led by a popular Islamic movement and based upon clear-cut objectives, well-designed methods, and fortitude.

However, the Sharī'ah justifies—even requires—silence on seeing *munkar*(evil), if it will lead to a greater *munkar.* This is in keeping with the Islamic axiom that a Muslim can choose to endure a lesser evil lest a greater one may result thereof. Such a choice is sanctioned by the Qur'ān, and is especially obvious in the story of Mūsā ('AS)[24] and his brother, Hārūn ('AS), who were commissioned to preach the divine message to Pharoah and his people. Mūsā ('AS) ascended Mount Sinai and left his people with Hārūn ('AS) as deputy. But as soon as Mūsā ('AS) had left, the Israelites began to worship a golden image of a calf, as was suggested to them by the Sāmirī, and refused to listen to Hārūn's dissuasions against such deviation.

> Hārūn had already, before this said to them: "O my people! You are being tested in this: for verily your Lord is Most Gracious: so follow me and obey my command." They had said "We will not abandon this cult, but we will devote ourselves to it until Mūsā returns to us (20:90-91).

Finding them adamant, however, Hārūn ('AS) kept silent. When Mūsā ('AS) returned and discovered the deviation of his people, he was angered and full of grief, rebuked Hārūn ('AS) and was very rough with him:

> "O Hārūn! What kept you back, when you saw them going wrong, from following me? Did you then disobey my order?" (20:93).

---

[24] *'Alayhi al Salām or 'Alayhim al Salam*: "Upon him (or them) be the blessing of [Allah]:" Said whenever a prophet other than Muḥammad (ṢA'AS) is mentioned by name.

Hārūn ('AS) replied:

> "O son of my mother! Seize [me] not by my beard nor by [the hair of] my head. Truly I feared lest you should say: 'You have caused a division among the children of Israel, and you did not respect my words!' " (20:94).

Hārūn ('AS) considered the preservation of the unity of the community until its leader returned—so that he would not be accused of taking a hasty decision and of initiating—discord, a good reason for his silence. This is relevant to the ḥadīth, mentioned earlier, in which the Prophet (ṢA'AS) said that he would have destroyed the old Ka'bah and rebuilt it on the foundations laid down by Ibrāhīm ('AS) but for his consideration of the fact that his followers had only recently abandoned their paganism.

Other examples are to be found in the Prophet's command to Muslims to endure the injustice of their rulers if they do not have the power to oust them and replace them with righteous ones, lest this should create an even greater *fitnah* and discord and lead to catastrophic results, such as the shedding of Muslim blood, the loss of property, and instability, without having achieved any tangible result. Such rulers may therefore be tolerated unless, of course, the condition reaches a clear-cut deviation and *kufr* or *riddah*. The Prophet (ṢA'AS) said in this respect: "Unless you witness open *kufr* for which you have evidence from Allah."[25]

Both instances clearly demonstrate the importance of maintaining unity in the face of an uncertain success. On the other hand, it is instructive to the dreamy idealists who want Muslims either to be absolutely perfect in observing Islamic teachings or to leave the fold of Islam altogether. For them there is simply no midway. In the opinion of such idealists, physical force is the only method which should be used to change *munkar*, overlooking the other two ways: with words and with the heart; and that all this depends on the ability and circumstances of the individual. They seem to have forgotten the fact that Islam does not sanction overburdening people whose different abilities and circumstances must always be taken into consideration. The Sharī'ah has certainly taken into consideration different circumstances and certain necessities to the extent that in compelling circumstances, the prohibited becomes lawful and the *wājib* is abrogated. Ibn Taymīyah's discussion of this is very apt. He writes:

> Allah (SWT) has told us in many places [in the Qur'ān] that

[25] Reported by al Bukhārī and Muslim.

He places no burden on people greater than that which they are capable of. He said: "On no soul does Allah place a burden greater than it can bear" (2:286). Also: "But those who believe and do righteousness, no burden do We place on any soul but that which it can bear" (7:42), and: "No soul shall have a burden laid on it greater than it can bear" (2:233), as well as: "Allah puts no burden on any person beyond what He has given him" (65:7).

Allah has also commanded man to obey Him as best he can. He said: "So heed Allah as much as you can" (64:16). The believers themselves have prayed to Him: "Our Lord! Lay not on us a burden like that which You laid on those before us. Our Lord! Lay not on us a burden greater than we have the strength to bear" (2:286). Allah (SWT) accepted their request. All these texts, therefore, show that He does not put a burden on a person which the latter cannot fulfill, contrary to the philosophy of the pre-determinist Jahamīyah; He does not punish those who fall into error or forget, contrary to the fatalist Qadarīyah, and the rationalist Mu'tazilah.

The point to be emphasized is that if a ruler, an imām, a scholar, a jurist, or a muftī, etc., excercises ijtihād to the best of his ability and with a genuine heal of Allah, his ijtihād is that which Allah has asked of him, and He will not be punished if his verdict is wrong. This is contrary to the pre-determined Jahamīyah who view a *mujtahid* as obedient to Allah but may or may not have reached the truth. This is contrary, also to both the Qadarīyah and the Mu'tazilah, who view all those exercising *ijtihad* to have reached the truth; their attitude in this regard is *bāṭil* (false).

The same is granted to the *kuffār*: those who received the Prophet's *da'wah* in the land of *kufr*, recognized him as the Messenger of Allah, believed in what was revealed to him, and obeyed Allah as best they could—like the Negus and others—but could not emigrate to the homeland of Islam and could not adhere to the totality of the Sharī'ah, either because they were not permitted to emigrate or because they were not allowed to practise their beliefs openly; and those who had no one to teach them Islamic Sharī'ah. All those are believers among the people of *Jannah, in shā'a Allāh*. Examples are the believer among the people of Pharaoh, the wife of Pharaoh, and Yūsuf the Truthful (ʿAS) who called the people of Egypt—who were *kuffār*—to *īmān* and monotheism although he was unable to tell them all that he knew about Islam. But they still refused to listen to him. In the Qur'an, the believer among the people of Pharaoh said to them: "And to you there came Yūsuf in times gone by, with clear signs, but you ceased not to doubt the mission for which he had come. At length, when he died, you said, "No apostle will Allah send after him" (40:34).

Moreover, although the Negus was the king of the Christians, they did not obey him when he asked them to embrace Islam. Only a small group followed him, and therefore, when he died there was no one to perform *ṣalāh* on him. However, the Prophet (ṢAʿAS) performed *ṣalāh* on him in Madīnah where a large number joined the *ṣalāh* as the Prophet (ṢAʿAS) told them of the Negus' death and said: "A righteous brother of yours from the people of Abyssinia has died,"[26] The Negus, however, was unable to adhere to a great number of the teachings of Islam, and he did not emigrate to the homeland of Islam, participate in jihād, nor perform *ḥajj*. It is also related that he did not perform the five *ṣalawāt*, nor *ṣiyām*, or give *zakāh*, because these would reveal his conviction to his people whom he could not go against. We know for sure that he could not apply on his people the judgments of the Qur'ān, although Allah has commanded His Messenger to apply these judgments on the People of the Book if they seek Him. Allah also warned the Prophet not to let the People of the Book persuade him to deviate from even part of what Allah has revealed to him.

ʿUmar ibn ʿAbd al ʿAzīz (RAʿA) encountered a great deal of animosity and suffering because of his unwavering commitment to justice. It is believed that he was poisoned because of this. However, the Negus and others like him are happy in *Jannah*, although they did not adhere except to that part of the Sharīʿah which they were able to, and although they applied the laws and judgment which were applicable.[27]

---

[26] Reported by Muslim.

[27] *Majmūʿ al Fatāwā*, 19:216-219.

5. Knowledge and Insight into the *Sunan* of Allah's Creation

Islam is the religion of rational and critical minds. This is why one of its fundamental goals is to make man aware of the paramount significance of gradation, fortitude, and maturity. Haste is an inherent characteristic of man in general, and of the young in particular. Indeed, haste is an outstanding characteristic of our own age. It has made our youth eager to saw the seeds today and to harvest the next day. But Allah's will in His own creation does not allow that: a tree goes through stages of growth, short or long, before it bears fruit. The very creation of a human being illustrates this very clearly:

> Then We made the sperm into a clinging clot; then of that clot We made a [foetus] lump; then We made out of that lump bones and clothed the bones with flesh; then We developed out of it another creature. So blessed be Allah, the best Creator (23:14).

A child is born, breast-fed and weaned, then he/she gradually grows from childhood to maturity. Similarly, life gradually moves from one stage to another until Allah's *sunan* (patterns) are realized. Islam began as a simple *dīn*, then gradually the obligatory duties were introduced, the prohibitions prescribed, and legislative matters detailed. Gradually, the structure took full shape, and Allah's favors and blessings were diffused everywhere. Then the following verse was revealed:

> This day have I perfected your religion for you, completed My favor upon you and have chosen for you Islam as your religion (5:3).

Such development and stages are plain enought, but they are rarely, if at all, observed or acknowledged.

The enthusiastic young people are outraged by the corruption that surrounds them as they witness, and daily live, the rapidly worsening condition of the Islamic Ummah. The common concern initiates group meetings; they undertake to put things right, to salvage what is worth keeping. But in their haste and enthusiasm, they lose clarity of vision, they begin to daydream and build castles in the air, believing that they can blot out all forms of corruption and falsehood in addition to establishing the ideal Islamic state overnight. They underestimate or disregard the incalculable obstacles and pitfalls that exceed their means and potential. Their dilemma is like that of the man who asked Ibn Sīrīn to interpret a dream for him: he dreamed that he was swimming on dry land, flying without wings. Ibn Sīrīn told him that he too was a man of too many dreams and wishes. 'Alī ibn Abū Ṭālib (RA'A) warned his son: ". . .and beware of relying on wishes, for they are the goods of fools."

It is common knowledge that corrupt realities cannot be changed by immature strategies based only upon good wishes and intentions. It is pertinent here to draw attention to an invaluable book: *Ḥattā Yughayyirū Mā fī Anfusihim* (Until They Change That Within Their Souls) written by the Syrian scholar Jawdat Sa'īd. The book discusses the "patterns of change of the soul and of society," and its title is derived from the following two Qur'ānic verses:

> Verily, never will Allah change the condition of a people until they change it themselves [with their own souls] (13:11).

And:

> Because Allah will never change the grace which He has bestowed on a people until they change what is in their [own] souls (8:53).

True to its title, this book is a deep social and psychological study in light of the teachings of the Qur'ān. One of the best parts of the author's introduction is the following:

> There are those among young Muslims who have the readiness and the determination to sacrifice their lives and wealth for the cause of Islam. Unfortunately, there are only a few among them who choose to spend their lives pursuing a serious research in order to perfect a particular discipline or clarify an obscure truth. For example, problems such as the dichotomy between belief and behavior, between what is professed and what is actually done. Such issues pose questions which badly need objective and well-informed answers without which any constructive reform is impossible. The sluggishness of existing studies is due to the fact that the Islamic world has not yet fully realized the importance or the necessity of research due to its common belief that: "The sword is mightier than the pen" rather than "Think before you leap." These different perceptions remain in total confusion;

neither the real relationships nor the natural order in them were studied or comprehended.

Moreover, the conditions of *īmān* have not yet been carefully studied in the Muslim world. This does not mean that Muslims have not learned the fundamentals of *īmān* and of Islam. But by this we mean the psychological conditions, i.e., that which must be changed within the soul, because this change brings about the fruition of *īmān*, that is, the condition of conformity between action and belief.

It is still believed that self-sacrifice and *ṣadaqah* are the highest of virtues without serious consideration of that which makes these so. Mere sacrifice cannot realize goals in the absence of its well-planned, well-thought strategies. This conception encourages young Muslims to sacrifice their lives and wealth yet fails to make them endeavor and persevere to study and to comprehend. Another reason is that self-sacrifice could result from a momentary impulse; but the pursuit of knowledge demands unflinching perseverence, consciousness, critical analysis, and insight, all of which ensure continuity and enhance success. Yet, many young Muslims enthusiastically embark upon deeds and studies in various fields, but after they start their enthusiasm begins to wane, they give way to boredom and eventually discontinue what they have started.

We must investigate these impending attitudes to discover the causes of such inalertness to, and discontinuity of, serious studies, all of which occur as a result of specific causes and factors which cannot be detected by hasty minds.

The trend to look for the hasty reform and change of reality in the absence of self-change and consciousness is equally absurd. Feeling the impact of the present reality on our condition is one thing, but consciousness of our own roles (i.e., that which is in ourselves) in perpetuating it is quite another. This is indeed what the Qur'ān seeks to teach humans by explaining what happens to them, and by emphasizing the following: that the core of the problem is "that which is in the self or the soul," not an external injustice. This is the essence of historical and social change which the Qur'ān sanctions. Failure to realize this plain truth blurs our vision and initiates those pessimistic and submissive, or despotic and non-Islamic, philosophies.

The gravest self-inflicted injustice is, indeed, the failure to perceive the inherent subservient relationship between man, the universe, and society. As a result, man misjudges his own abilities and fails to put himself where he can harness human and natural potential to advantage in accordance with the *sunan* inherent in these. Accordingly, we can say that two attitudes are open for the human mind when confronted with a problem: to believe that the problem is governed by certain patterns and can therefore be solved and controlled; or to believe that it is mysterious and supernatural and therefore not governed by any patterns, or that such patterns cannot be revealed. Between these two extremes there are numerous other intermediate attitudes: each hypothesis has a practical result which is relatively reflected in the attitudes and behavior of people depending on the direction they adopt.

The failure of Muslims to live in accordance with the teachings of Islam is a problem which is easily proved. Even when the problem is accepted, the question still remains: which of the foregoing attitudes should Muslims take? The discussion of the issue in such a way as to bring it to the awareness of the Muslim will help him to determine his attitude toward the problem and to abandon the ambiguous attitude which he might take. In many cases, when the two attitudes are entangled and therefore paralyze the effect of each other, the issues remain ambiguous. A solution requires, to a great extent, a sound hypothesis.

6. A Dialogue on the *Sunan* and Conditions of Victory

Below is the dialogue which took place between a young Muslim enthusiast and myself. He asked and I answered:

Q: Are we not following *ḥaqq* (truth) and our opponents following *bāṭil* (falsehood)?

A: Yes, indeed.

Q: Has not our Lord promised us that *ḥaqq* will triumph over *bāṭil*, and *īmān* over *kufr*?

A: Yes, and Allah (SWT) will never break His promise.

Q: So, what are we waiting for? Why do we not wage war against *bāṭil*?

A: Our religion instructs us that victory is governed by certain *sunan* and conditions to which we must adhere. Had it not been for such considerations, the Prophet (ṢA'AS) would have declared war on paganism at the beginning of the Makkan period. He would not have tolerated performing *ṣalāh* at the Ka'bah when it was surrounded by idols.

Q: What are these *sunan* and conditions?

A: First, Allah (SWT) does not make *ḥaqq* triumphant simply because it is so; but He makes it victorious through the united body of the righteous and brotherly people who believe in Allah *ta'ālā*. This is clear from the following verse:

> He it is that has strengthened you with His aid and with the believers, and has put affection in their hearts (8:62-63).

Q: But what about the angels who descended to aid *ḥaqq* against *bāṭil*, such as those who aided the believers during the battles of Badr, al Khandaq, and Ḥunayn?

A: The angels are there and will come to the rescue of the believers when Allah (SWT) so wills. However, they will not descend in a vacuum: there must be true believers down here on earth who strive to make *ḥaqq* prevail and who need aid from heaven to strengthen them. The Qur'ān is clear on this issue as is clear in the following verse which was revealed during the battle of Badr:

> Remember your Lord inspired the angels [with the message]: "I am with you. Give firmness to the believers. I will instill terror into the hearts of the unbelievers" (8:12).

Q: If there are true believers, would that ensure victory?

A: They have to spread Islam to the best of their abilities, multiply their numbers, and conduct dialogues with their opponents in the hope of convincing them of the truth of their claims. In this way they will obtain the power to encounter their enemies. It would be irrational for one single person to attempt to stand up against a hundred or a thousand. The maximum number mentioned in the Qur'ān of unbelievers that a true believer full of vigor and determination could stand up against is ten:

> O Prophet! rouse the believers to fight. If there are twenty among you, patient and persevering, they will vanquish two hundred; if a hundred, they will vanquish a thousand of the unbelievers (8:65).

But in times of weakness, the numbers are different:

> For the present, Allah has lightened your [task] for He knows that there is a weak spot in you: But [even so], if there are a hundred of you, patient and persevering, they will vanquish two hundred, and if a thousand, they will vanquish two thousand, with the leave of Allah. For Allah is with those who patiently persevere (8:66).

Q: But our adversaries are always on the alert; they have excelled in sabotaging our endeavors to spread the divine word.

A: This certifies the claim that there is an indispensible condition without which no victory can be guaranteed, i.e., patience in the face of suffering, perseverence in the face of defiance and provocation. The Prophet (ṢA'AS) told his cousin 'Abd Allah ibn 'Abbās that "Patience is a prerequisite of victory." This is also the advice of Allah (SWT) to His Prophet (ṢA'AS):

> Follow the inspiration sent unto you, and be patient and constant until Allah decides, for He is the Best to decide (10:109).

And in another verse:

> And be patient, for your patience is but from Allah, nor grieve over them, and do not distress yourself because of their plots, for Allah is with those who restrain themselves and those who do good (16:127-128).

Also:

> So patiently persevere, for verily the promise of Allah is true. Nor let those who have [themselves] no certainty of faith shake your firmness (30:60).

And:

> And therefore patiently persevere, as did [all] messengers of inflexible purpose; and be in no haste about the [unbelievers] (46:35).

And again:

> Now await in patience the command of your Lord, for verily

> you are in Our eyes, and celebrate the praises of your Lord while you stand forth (52:48).

Q: But we may patiently persevere for too long without ever succeeding in establishing an Islamic state which will apply the Sharī'ah, resurrect the Muslim Ummah, and once again raise the banner of Islam.

A: But, do you not in the meantime instruct an ignorant person, guide someone to the right path, or lead another to repent? When he answered in the affirmative, I added: This is a tremendous achievement which brings us closer to our goal. The Prophet (ṢA'AS) said: "If Allah enables you to guide one person [to the Straightforward Path] it is better for you than all the best breed of camel [you may possess]." Furthermore, the obligatory duty which we will be asked to account for is to make *da'wah,* to instruct and work, but not necessarily to achieve our aims ourselves. We must sow love and pray to Allah (SWT) for a great harvest. The Qur'ān indeed, instructs us:

> And say: "Work [righteousness]: Soon will Allah observe your work and His messenger, and the believers. Soon you will be brought back to the Knower of what is hidden and what is open. Then will He show you the truth of all that you did" (9:105).

CHAPTER FOUR

Advice to Muslim Youth

At the end of my previously mentioned study published in *al Ummah,* in which I discussed the positive as well as the negative aspects of the "Reawakening of Muslim Youth," I emphasized two facts:

First:

That this resurgence signifies a natural, healthy phenomenon which is clearly indicative of a return to *fiṭrah* (inborn nature), to the roots, which—for us in our Muslim homeland—is simply Islam: the beginning and the end, into which we seek refuge from difficulties, and from which we derive a strength of spirit, of hope, and of guidance. Our Muslim communities have tried solutions imported from either the West or the East, but all have failed to bring about any spiritual elevation, material prosperity, goodness, or social welfare in any Muslim country. On the contrary, the adoption of these imported alien systems has involved us in a labyrinth of difficulties which have generated disunity and disintegration in the Muslim communities. As a result, public opinion now firmly believes in the inevitability of the Islamic solution, i.e., the application of Sharī'ah in all aspects of life. It is not surprising, therefore, that the role of young Muslims in this endeavor is characterized by courage, determination, and resolve.

Second:

The manifestations of rigidity and strictness in some of our youth cannot be rectified by violence, threats, or allegations which will be counterproductive and may lead to more severity and stubbornness. None of us can doubt the good intentions and sincerity of the youth towards Allah (SWT) and themselves. Therefore, such manifestations can only be remedied by identifying with the young, by understanding their attitudes and thinking, by showing goodwill toward their intentions and aim by bridging the gap between them and the rest of society, by conducting patient intellectual dialogues with them in order to clarify conceptions, to clear up misunderstandings, and to identify similarities and differences.

In pursuance of such dialogues, I have given much advice to Muslim youths. In doing so, I sought nothing but Allah's pleasure. Believers—

the Prophet (ṢA'AS) taught us – should always consult with and advise one another, commanding the common good and forbidding evil and undesirable things with patience and with perserverance. These are necessary requisites for achieving success in this life and rewards in the hereafter. My advice however, is intended to be a landmark which will, *in shā'a Allāh,* lead us toward our goal, enable us to avoid pitfalls and deviation, and ensure the continuity of our march. Below are some extracts:

> The young are advised to respect specialization. We live in an age in which specialization has become essential; excelling in one discipline does not necessarily mean excelling in another. Just as a physician cannot be consulted on engineering matters, or a physician on law, it is wrong to consider Sharī'ah open to the interpretation of all people by claiming that knowledge of *fiqh* and Islam, cannot be monopolized by a special group of people, and that Islam, unlike other religions, does not recognize the existence of a class of clergy, or *rijāl al dīn.* It is true that Islam has never known such a class as the Christian clergy, but it fully recognizes the role assigned to scholars specialized in religious matters and referred to in the following Qur'ānic verse:
>
> Nor should the believers all go forth together. If a contingent from every expedition remained behind, they could devote themselves to studies in religion, and admonish the people when they return to them, that thus they [may learn] to guard themselves [against evil] (9:122).

The Qur'ān and *Sunnah* teach us to refer matters of which we have no knowledge to the learned and the experienced:

> Before you, also, the messengers We sent were but men to whom We granted inspiration. If you realise this not, ask of those who possess the Message (21:7).

And:

> When there comes to them some matter touching [public] safety or fear, they divulge it. If they had only referred it to the Messenger, or to those charged with authority among them, the proper investigators would have tested it from them [direct] (4:83).

Also:

> Ask then, about Him of any acquainted [with such things] (25:59).

In another verse He says:

> And none [O man!] can tell you [the Truth] like the one who is acquainted with all things (35:14).

The Prophet (ṢA'AS) also said, when he was informed that a wounded man was given a *fatwā* that he must wash the whole of his body before performing ablution and *ṣalāh* which resulted in his death: "They caused his death, may Allah cause their death [as well]. Should not they have asked if they were not sure. . .?"

It was indeed shocking to discover that there are people who, even though totally unqualified, are only too ready to give *fatāwā* on the most serious and complex issues: *fatāwā* which may contradict those of both earlier and contemporary *'ulamā'.* Such people may never hesitate to dismiss as wrong the *fatāwā* of other scholars whom they accuse of ignorance, claiming that the gates of ijtihād are not exclusive to a special few but are open to all. This is true, but itjihād requires certain requisites of which such people possess none. Our predecessors have criticized even some of the learned who hastened to give *fatwā* without careful consideration and knowledge of the matter saying: "Some people hastily give *fatwā* on matters which, if referred to 'Umar ibn al Khaṭṭāb, would have caused him to consult all the people [who took part in the battle] of Badr," and also, "The most daring among you in giving *fatwā* is the most daring [to commit sins which will cause them] to [be sent to] the Fire."

Despite the profound depth of knowledge of the Rightly-Guided Caliphs, they used to consult and be consulted by their learned companions when confronted with critical issues. Out of the body of *fatāwā* which were made collectively emerged the *ijma'* (consensus) in the first Islamic era. When consulted, some companions refrained from making any comment, and others simply used to say that they did not know. 'Utbah ibn Muslim reported that he was once Ibn 'Umar's companion for a period of thirty-four months. During that time, Ibn 'Umar was asked about various important issues and he often replied that he did not know. Ibn Abū Laylā related the following about at least 120 companions of the Prophet (ṢA'AS), most of whom were from among the *Anṣār* and were his contemporaries:

When one of them was consulted on a certain issue, he would refer the questioner to another, who in turn would refer him to another and so on until the questioner finally returns to the first person whom he had approached first. They wished to be spared the reporting of a hadith or giving a *fatwa* in answer to a question.

Furthermore, 'Aṭā' ibn al Ṣā'ib said that he observed many of his contemporaries tremble whenever giving *fatwā*. Among *the Tābi'ūn*, Sa'īd ibn al Musayyib—who excelled them all in *fiqh*—rarely gave *fatwā*. But when he had to, he used to pray to Allah (SWT) to save him if he was unintentionally wrong and to save those who would follow his *fatwā*.

The same caution is observed repeatedly in the practice of the *a'immah* of the followed *madhāhib*. It was the rule rather than the exception for them to reply that they did not know when they were uncertain. Al Imām Mālik, for instance, was exceptionally cautious and used to say: "If a person is asked about a certain issue, he should think of *jannah* and of *jahannam*[1] and of his own salvation in the hereafter before he replies." Ibn al Qāsim also heard Mālik saying: "I have been investigating a particular issue for more than ten years, but I have not made up my mind about it yet." Ibn Mahdī also heard Mālik saying: "Sometimes a matter is brought to me [to investigate], and I spend the whole night in [contemplating] it." Moreover, Muṣ'ab related that his father was once consulted on a certain issue but, uncertain, he asked his son to take the questioner to Mālik whose reply was: "I cannot tell, go and ask those who know better." Ibn Abū Ḥasan said: "Mālik was consulted on twenty-one issues, but he only gave *fatwā* on two of them, repeating several times after that: 'There is neither strength nor power except what is given by Allah.'"

It is indeed not my intention to discourage young Muslims from the pursuit of knowledge and learning. To learn is an obligation which is enjoined upon us from the cradle to the grave. But what I intend to emphasize here is that however broad their learning and knowledge may be, they are bound to heed those who are specialized. The Sharī'ah has various interdisciplinary branches and *uṣūl* which these young Muslims are incapable of knowing or comprehending and for which they neither have the time nor the means. Furthermore, I feel obliged to point out that I do not approve of the tendency of some youths who abandon the colleges

---

[1] *Jahannam*: "The eternal fire which is the ultimate recompense of the life of disobedience and sin."

in which they have enrolled, and in which they have made good progress and are expected to do well, and seek to specialize in Sharī'ah. Such people ignore the fact that to pursue knowledge—and to excel in any discipline—is *farḍ kifāyah:* a collective obligation. It should also be observed that the competition between Muslims and non-Muslims for mastery of the secular sciences is at its highest. When a Muslim seeks to learn, to excel, and acquire insight into such sciences for the sake of Allah (SWT) he is actually performing *'ibādah* and *jihād*.

Let us remember that when the divine message was revealed to the Prophet (ṢA'AS), his earlier companions had various professions. The Prophet (ṢA'AS) did not ask them to give up their work and devote themselves to the study of Islam, except, of course, those who were entrusted with a special mission and who had to adjust themselves to its fulfillment. What I honestly fear is that the tendency to give up pursuing other disciplines in order to study and master Sharī'ah may be motivated by an unconscious covert desire for popularity, ostentation, and leadership, especially in meetings, debates and seminars. Such a desire is not easy to detect, because Satan has countless means and inlets into the human soul which is vulnerable to temptation, unless that individual is constantly alert. This means that we should carefully investigate our thoughts, motivations and strategies; we should constantly try to find out whether these are impelled by mundane or spiritual goals. Self-deception is a snare which confuses motives and blurs clarity of vision. We should never tire of reminding ourselves of this Qur'ānic verse: "Whoever holds firmly to Allah will be shown a Way that is straight" (3:101).

Since every discipline is best known by those who are specialized in it, the young are strongly advised to acquire religious knowledge from trustworthy scholars who have combined depth of knowledge with piety, righteousness, and balance in their own lives. The main sources of Islamic knowledge are the Qur'ān and *Sunnah*, but whoever desires to enrich his understanding and knowledge of both cannot do so without the interpretations of the *'ulamā',* the explanation of scholar, and the comprehension of the *fuqahā'* who have devoted their lives to the study of both and who originated *uṣūl al fiqh*, thereby transmitting to us a legacy which only the ignorant and the arrogant can disregard. A person who boasts of possessing knowledge of the Qur'ān and *Sunnah*, but despises the knowledge handed down to us by our learned predecessors, cannot be entrusted with the teachings of Islam. On the other hand, a person who only draws upon the findings of *'ulamā'* and *fuqahā',* as well as the works of the four great jurists of Islam, but brushes aside the evidence and indications of the Qur'ān and Ḥadith, ignores the source of faith and legislation.

There are scholars who specialize in a single branch of Islamic culture not directly related to the Qur'ān and *Sunnah*, such as history, philosophy, and Sufism. These can be useful in their special fields, but they are not qualified to give *fatāwā* or to teach Sharī'ah to others. Some of these may be born orators and preachers and are able to eloquently persuade others, but this does not qualify them for scholarly investigation, because they often mix truth with myth, the genuine with the false, the significant with the insignificant. They give wrong *fatāwā* on matters not fully comprehended by them. They confuse issues and priorities, unduly exaggerate or underestimate matters. However, people who are enchanted by their style and eloquence unhesitantly accept their verdicts and opinions. Thus we need to be reminded that rhetoric is one thing and *fiqh* is another, and that the person who excels in one does not necessarily excel in the other.

Furthermore, a person who does not practice what he preaches is not worthy of teaching or guiding people. Practice is manifested in righteousness, piety, and the consciousness of Allah (SWT), which are the fruits of genuine knowledge. The Qur'ān says: "Those who truly fear Allah among His servants are those who have knowledge" (35:28). Such piety and heeding of Allah (SWT) prevent a Muslim scholar from indulging ignorantly in religious issues unknown to him, or from serving—through his knowledge—a specific ruler or regime.

A third characteristic to be observed in a truly learned person is balance, which is also a unique quality of Islam. We have been unfortunate in this age to witness opposing groups of people who claim knowledge: the excessive and the negligent, the extremist and the rejectionist. Al Ḥasan al Baṣrī warned us that "religion will be lost as a result of the practice of both the excessive and the negligent." The former tend to prohibit almost everything while the latter make everything lawful and permissible.

Some extremists adhere to one *madhhab* and seek to seal the gates of ijtihād. On the other hand, the lax and negligent defame all *madhāhib* and endeavor to refute all doctrines and verdicts embodied therein. There are also the literalists who adhere to the literal interpretation of texts without any consideration for the purpose or rules, and at the other end those who interpret the contents of the texts according to their own whims and desires. In between the two extremes the issues are lost. We therefore need those balanced people who have the mind of a *faqīh* and the heart of a pious man; those who reconcile duties with reality, who distinguish clearly between what is to be expected from the less committed and what is to be expected of the committed, and know full well that necessities have their exceptional rules, and that in seeking facilitation one must not remove the barriers between the lawful and the prohibited, or, being too cautious, cause difficulties and hardships for people. Al Imām Sufyān al Thawrī, well known for his piety and his profound knowledge of Ḥadīth and *fiqh*, said: "[Regarding the Commandments of prohibition in Islam] dispensations and licenses should be sought from a trustworthy *fiqih;* but strict *fatawah* can be prescribed by anyone!"

Young Muslims are advised to eschew excessiveness and extremism and to commit themselves to temperance and facilitation, especially in dealing with the lay people who are not expected to react as the righteous and pious do. A Muslim can, if he so wishes, adhere to a cautious stand on one issue or on a number of issues. But if he always disregards religious facilitation in favor of caution and circumspection, Islam will ultimately turn into a "set of precautions" manifest only by strictness and difficulties, although Allah (SWT) enjoins facilitation and spaciousness for His servants. Indeed the Qur'ān, *Sunnah,* and the practices of the Prophet's companions all call for facilitation and warn against excessiveness and against making things too difficult for the believers. The following Qur'ānic verses, on the subjects of *ṣiyām*; cleanliness, marriage, and *qiṣāṣ*[2], respectively, demonstrate this point:

> Allah intends every facility for you; He does not want to put you to difficulties (2:185).
>
> Allah does not wish to place you in a difficulty (5:6).
>
> Allah does wish to lighten your [difficulties] for man was created weak [in flesh] (4:28).
>
> O you who believe! The law of equality is prescribed to you in cases of murder: the free for the free, the slave for the slave, the woman for the woman. But if any remission is made by the brother [of the slain], then grant any reasonable demand and compensate him with handsome gratitude. This is a concession and a mercy from your Lord. (2:178).

With regard to *Sunnah,* reference has already been made to several

---

[2] *Qiṣāṣ*: "The law of equality of punishment".

aḥādīth which recommend moderation and balance and warn against excessiveness in religion:

> Beware of excessiveness in religion. [People] before you have perished as a result of [such] excessiveness.[3]

> "Ruined are those who indulge in *ṭanaṭu'* (hairsplitting)." And the Prophet (ṢA'AS) repeated the above *ḥadīth* thrice.[4]

In addition, Abū Hurayrah related the following:

> A bedouin once urinated in the *masjid*. The people rushed to punish him, but the Prophet (ṢA'AS) ordered them: "Leave him alone and pour a bucket of water or tumbler of water [over the place where he has urinated]. Your mission is to make things easy and not to make them difficult."[5]

It is true that whenever the Prophet (ṢA'AS) had to choose between two options he always chose the easiest, unless it was a sin.[6] He also addressed Mu'ādh (RA'A) when he heard that the latter prolonged *ṣalāh*: "O Mu'ādh! Are you putting the people on trial?"[7] The Prophet (ṢA'AS) repeated this thrice to emphasize that creating difficulties for people or attempting to use force with them always leads to *fitnah* (discord, dissuasion from one's Islamic commitments).

Moreover, a person may – in seeking perfection and caution – have the right to make things difficult for himself, but he should not impose or force the same on other people and therefore unconsciously alienate them from religion. For this reason, the Prophet (ṢA'AS) used to prolong *ṣalāh* whenever he was alone and to shorten it whenever he led others. He said in this respect:

> Whoever among you leads the people in *ṣalāh*, he should shorten it, for amongst them are the weak, the sick, the old, and the one who has business to attend to. And if anyone among you performs *ṣalāh* alone, he then may prolong [*ṣalāh*] as much as he wishes.[8]

Al Bukhārī reported that the Prophet (ṢA'AS) said: "As I start *ṣalah* I wish to prolong it, but as soon as I hear the crying of a child I shorten

---

3 Reported by Aḥmad, al Nasā'ī, and Ibn Mājah in their *Sunan*.
4 Reported by Muslim.
5 Reported by al Bukhārī.
6 Agreed upon by all authorities.
7 Reported by al Bukhārī.
8 Reported by al Bukhārī.

it so as to make it easier for the child's mother". Muslim reported in his *Ṣaḥīḥ*[9] that the Prophet (ṢA'AS) used to recite—when leading people in *ṣalāh*—short rather than long verses from the Qur'ān, 'Ā'ishah (RA'A) also said: "As a gesture of compassion, the Prophet (ṢA'AS) warned people against *wiṣāl* [i.e., joining successive days in *ṣiyām*]. But the people said to him: 'You do that.' He said: 'I am not like you. My Lord gives me food and drink.'"

The tendency to make matters easy is more urgently needed at this time than ever before. We live in an age which is immersed in materialism, lost in distractions, full of evils so overwhelming that the person who sticks to his religious principles faces a great deal of difficulty and stricture. This is the reason why the *fuqahā'* have approved of facilitation in times of hardships and trying calamities.

In calling non-Muslims to Islam and when conducting dialogues with them young Muslims are advised to follow the approach which has already been outlined for them. Several verses can be cited in this respect:

> Invite [all] to the Way of your Lord with wisdom and nice preaching, and argue with them in ways that are best and most gracious (16:125).

Evidently, the above verse commands not only "nice preaching" but also "the most gracious." Therefore, if there are two ways to conduct a dialogue, the best should be adopted in order to win people's hearts and to bridge gaps. One of the best ways is that on which points of agreement are first mentioned and discussed leading to the points of disagreement. The Qur'ān states:

> And dispute not with the People of the Book, except with means better [than mere disputation], unless it be with those of them who inflict wrong [and injury]. But say "We believe in the revelation which has come down to us and in that which came down to you. Our God and your God is one, and it is to Him that we bow [in Islam]" (29:46).

Any remaining points of disagreement will be judged by Allah (SWT):

> If they wrangle with you, say: "Allah knows best what it is you are doing. Allah will judge between you on the Day of Judgment concerning the matters on which you differ" (22:68-69).

---

[9] *Al Ṣaḥīḥ*: "Any of the six collections of *aḥādīth* widely regarded as trustworthy—namely, those of al Bukhārī, Muslim, al Sijistānī, al Tirmidhī, al Nasā'ī, and Ibn Mājah.

If this is the way a Muslim is required to conduct a dialogue with a non-Muslim, how then should a Muslim talk to his Muslim brother with whom he shares this great *dīn?* Some of our Muslim brothers confuse frankness and harshness in expressing the truth, although the two are unrelated. A sagacious *dāʿīyah* is he who conveys and communicates the message to others in a gentle manner and in the "most gracious" terms without, of course, compromising the content of his message. Factual evidence should teach us that the content, no matter how great it is, is likely to be distorted and lost through a harsh approach. This is why it was said: "He who commands the common good should do it with common sense."

Al Imām al Ghazālī wrote in his book, *Al Amr bi al Maʿrūf wa al Nahī ʿan al Munkar*: "A person commanding the common good and forbidding that which is evil and undesirable should show compassion, sympathy, wisdom, and knowledge." To demonstrate this he related the story of a man who came upon al Ma'mūn, the prominent ʿAbbāsī caliph, and started to "counsel" him about vice and virtue in a rough and crude manner with no consideration for his status. Al Ma'mūn, who had a good knowledge of *fiqh*, addressed the man: "Speak more kindly. Remember that Allah has sent someone better than you to a ruler worse than me, and commanded the former to speak mildly; he has sent Mūsā and Hārūn, who were better than you, to Pharaoh, who was worse than me, and commanded them:

> 'Go, both of you, to Pharaoh, for he has indeed transgressed all bounds, but speak to him mildly. Perchance he may take warning or fear [Allah]' '(20:43-44).

Thus, al Ma'mūn was able to give his critic a significant advice. Moreover, Allah (SWT) has also taught Mūsā (ʿAS) that his message to Pharaoh should be delivered in such a mild gentle way:

> Go to Pharaoh, for he has indeed trangressed all bounds; and say to him, would you want to be purified [from sin]?—and that I guide you to your Lord, so you should fear Him? (79:17-19).

Further examination of the dialogue between Mūsā (ʿAS) and Pharaoh—as related in the Qur'ān—reveals that the former has carried out very carefully Allah's advice, despite the latter's tyranny, arrogance, insults, accusations, and attacks, as evident in *Sūrat al Shuʿarā'* (26).

A study of the Prophet's life and his Sunnah which pertains to this theme also reveals kindness, mercy, and mildness, which allows no place for roughness, cruelty, or hardheartedness. The Qur'ān describes the Prophet's attitude in this regard:

> Now has come unto you a Messenger from among yourselves.
> It grieves him that you should perish and ardently anxious
> is he over you. To the believers he is most kind and merciful
> (9:128).

It also describes the Prophet's relationship with his companions:

> It is part of the mercy of Allah that you deal gently with them.
> If you were severe or hardhearted, they would have broken
> away from you (3:159).

One day, a group of Jews came upon the Prophet (ṢAʿAS) and greeted him with: *al sāmu ʿalaykum* which literally means "death be upon you" instead of the usual *al salāmu ʿalaykum*. ʿĀ'ishah (RAʿA) was angered by this and replied: *ʿalaykum al sāmu wa al laʿnah* (death and curse be on you). But the Prophet (ṢAʿAS) said no more than *"wa ʿalaykum"* (and upon you). He then turned to ʿĀ'ishah (RAʿA) and said: "Allah loves that one should be kind in all matters."[10] ʿĀ'ishah also related another hadith: "Allah is kind and He loves kindness; and confers upon kindness that which he does not confer upon severity, and does not confer upon anything else beside it [kindness]"[11] Also: "Kindness makes things beautiful, absence of kindness makes them defective."[12]

Jarir ibn ʿAbd Allah related that he heard the Prophet (ṢAʿAS) say: "He who is deprived of tender feelings is in fact deprived of all good."[13] What other punishment could be harder than being deprived of all good?

Hopefully, these Islamic texts are sufficient enough to convince those youths who follow offensive and violent means that they must eschew the violence, excessiveness, and extremism which have become their characteristics and follow the path of wisdom, amicability, and tolerance.

I would like here to emphasize several relevant and important points in the ethics of *daʿwah* and dialogue:

1. Parental and kinship rights must be observed. Neither parents nor brothers and sisters should be treated with coarseness or disrespect on the grounds that they are transgressors, innovators, or deviants. These failings do not cancel their rights for kind and lenient treatment. Paren-

---

[10] Agreed upon by all authorities.

[11] Reported by Muslim.

[12] Reported by Muslim.

[13] Reported by Muslim in this inclusive manner.

tal rights in particular are categorically expressed in the Qur'ān:

> But if they strive to make you join in worship with Me things of which you have no knowledge, obey then not; yet bear them company in this life with justice [and consideration], and follow the way of those who turn to Me [in love] (31:15).

Similarly, one can learn a great deal from prophet Ibrāhīm's gentle and persuasive approach—as illustrated in the Qur'ān[14]—in trying to lead his polytheist father to the Truth. Ibrāhīm persevered in his tender solicitude despite his father's brusque and repellent tone. What then if the parents were Muslims and kind? Even if they violate some injuctions of the Sharī'ah, they are still entitled to parental as well as Islamic rights.

2. Islam teaches the equality of all human beings, but this should not be confused and misunderstood. There are certain differences, such as age, which must be observed and which require us to show politeness and respect. We must indeed observe the rights of relatives, spouses, neighbors, and rulers. Islamic ethics teach us that the young must respect the old, that the old must show compassion toward the young. There are many *aḥādīth* which command such attitudes: "Respect for an old Muslim is a glorification of Allah;"[15] and: "A person who does not show compassion to the young, respect to the old, and gratitude to the learned is not one of us."[16]

3. Consideration must be given to those people who have rich experience and who were very active in the field of *da'wah*. If—for one reason or another—they become slack and lose their enthusiasm, we must not forget their contribution and not defame or discredit them. This is the Sunnah of the Prophet (ṢA'AS), as evident in the story of Ḥāṭīb ibn Abū Balta'ah, who sent a message to the pagans of Quraysh requesting protection for his children and relatives left behind in Makkah in return for information about the Muslims' strategy and weaponry being prepared to conquer Makkah. When the message was intercepted and Ḥāṭib confessed, 'Umar ibn al Khaṭṭāb (RA'A) was so outraged with this treachery that he requested the Prophet (ṢA'AS) to let him cut off Ḥāṭib's head. But the Prophet (ṢA'AS) refused, saying: "How do you know; perhaps

---

[14] See *Sūrat Maryam*.

[15] Reported by Abū Dāwūd on the authority of Mūsā with an authentic *īsnād*, as mentioned in al Manāwī's *tafsīr*, 1:347.

[16] Reported by Aḥmad on the authority of Ibn al Ṣāmit with authentic *isnād*. Also reported by al Ṭabarānī and al Ḥākim.

Allah has looked at [the deeds of] the people [who fought in the battle] of Badr and said to them: 'Do whatever you please for I have forgiven you [your past and future sins].'" Ḥāṭib's early embrace of Islam and his courage and struggle during the battle of Badr made the Prophet (ṢAʿAS) accept his excuse, thus reminding his companions—and indeed all Muslims—of the special status of those who fought in the battle of Badr—the first battle between the Muslims and the *kuffār*.

4. I advise the young to abandon their daydreams and their unrealistic idealism. They must come down to earth and identify with the masses, those who live from hand to mouth in the downtrodden parts of the big cities and in the impoverished and totally forgotten villages. In such places one can find the uncorrupted sources of virtue, simplicity, and purity in spite of "necessity's sharp pinch." There one can find the potential for social change, the opportunities for effort, struggle, movement, help, and reconstruction; there one can mix with the masses and show kindness and compassion towards the needy, the orphaned, the brokenhearted, the weary, and the oppressed. The realization of such objectives, which is in itself a form of *ʿibādah,* requires collective effort, the formation of committees dedicated to eradicating illiteracy, diseases, unemployment, lack of initiative, and harmful habits, i.e., addiction to smoking, alcohol, and drugs; and on the other hand, to exposing and fighting corruption, deviation, oppression, bribery, and other practices. The struggle to relieve the suffering of the poor and to provide them with proper guidance is indeed a suitable form of *ʿibādah*, the significance of which many Muslims are unaware, even though Islamic teachings not only encourage the propagation of charitable deeds but commend them as individual and collective duties.[17]

Charitable deeds done for the welfare of the community are the best forms of *ʿibādah* and are considered branches of *īmān*, as long as those who do them do not seek praise and cheap popularity but only the pleasure of Allah (SWT). Let us remind ourselves of those *aḥādīth* in which we learn that several acts, ranging from commanding the common good and forbidding the evil and the undesirable to simply removing harmful things from a path way, are all charitable deeds. Abū Hurayrah relates the following ḥadīth:

> *Ṣadaqah* is due on each joint of a person, every day the sun rises. The administration of justice between two men is also

[17] More detailed information on this theme can be found in al Qaraḍāwī, Y. *Al ʿIbādah fī al Islām.*

a *ṣadaqah*; assisting a man to mount his beast i.e., donkey, horse, camel, etc.], or helping him load his luggage upon it is a *ṣadaqah*; and a good word is a *ṣadaqah*; and every step taken towards *ṣalāh* is a *ṣadaqah*, removing harmful things from a pathway is *ṣadaqah*.[18]

Ibn 'Abbās (RA'A) also related another *ḥadīth* to the same effect:

> A *ṣalāh* is due on each joint of a person every day. A man in the audience said: "This is the most difficult thing you have required of us." The Prophet (ṢA'AS) then said: "Your commanding the common good and forbidding that which is evil and undesirable is a *ṣalāh*, your help for the weak is a *ṣalāh*, your removing of dirt from a pathway is *ṣalāh*, and every step you take to the [prescribed daily] *ṣalāh* is *ṣalāh*."[19]

Buraydah (RA'A) related that the Prophet (ṢA'AS) said:

> "A man has three hundred and sixty joints. He must give *ṣadaqah* for each one of them." They [the Prophet's companions] said: "Who can afford to do so, O Apostle?" thinking that it was a financial *ṣadaqah*. The Prophet (ṢA'AS) then said: "Heaping earth upon some phlegm in a *masjid* is *ṣadaqah*, removing an obstruction from a pathway is *ṣadaqah* . . ."[20]

There are many *aḥādīth* which rank cheerfulness towards other Muslims, helping the blind, the deaf and the weak, advising those who are lost and confused, relieving the distress of the needy, etc., as forms of *'ibādah* and *ṣadaqah*. In this way, a Muslim lives his life as a vital source of virtuous deeds, either performing good or commanding it upon others, thereby guarding against the infiltration of evil. The Prophet (ṢA'AS) said: "Blessed is he whom Allah has made a key for righteousness and a lock against evil."[21]

However some enthusiastic idealists may argue that such social activities would hinder the propagation of Islam and the efforts to make people understand it. They believe that Islamic education is more obligatory than these social engagements". My reply is that social involvement is itself a practical *da'wah* which reaches the people in their own environment. Calling people to Islam is not mere talk; *da'wah* is participation

---

[18] Agreed upon by all authorities.

[19] Reported by Ibn Khuzaymah in his *Ṣaḥīḥ*.

[20] Reported by Aḥmad, Abū Dāwūd, Ibn Khuzaymah, and Ibn Ḥibbān.

[21] Reported by Ibn Mājah.

in the affairs of others and the seeking of a remedy to their problems. Al Imām Ḥasan al Bannā was quite aware of this and therefore established a charitable institution for social services and financial assistance in every branch of the Muslim Brotherhood he founded in Egypt to call for Islam. He was conscious that the Muslim is commanded to do charitable work just as he is commanded to bow down and to prostrate himself in *'ibādah* for Allah (SWT). The Qur'ān says:

> O you who believe! Bow down, prostrate yourselves and adore your Lord and do good that you may prosper. And strive in His cause as you ought to strive [with sincerity and under discipline]. He has chosen you, and has imposed no difficulties on you in religion (22:77-78).

The above defines the Muslim's three-part role in this life: his relationship with Allah (SWT) Whom he should serve through *'ibādah*; his role in society which he should severe through charitable deeds; his relationship with the powers of darkness and evil against which he should wage *jihād*. But enthusiastic idealists might further argue that efforts should be concentrated on the establishment of an Islamic state which applies Sharī'ah in all aspects of life within the state and works to call for Islam outside its borders. The realization of this goal, they argue, will automatically solve all the foregoing problems. The establishment of an Islamic state which applies Sharī'ah and strives to unite all Muslims under the banner of Islam is, of course, the duty of the whole Ummah. All *du'āh* must do their utmost to achieve this objective, employing in the process the best means and methods. But the realization of this is conditional upon a number of imperatives, some of the most important of which are: to unite all efforts, to remove all obstacles, to convince the suspecting minds of the nobility of the cause, to bring up Islamically-orientated youngsters, and to prepare local as well as international public opinion to accept their ideology and their state. All this requires time and, indeed, perserverance. Until that dear hope is realized, Muslims must unite efforts in order to serve their communities and to improve their societies. Such engagements will mold, prepare, and test the abilities of future generations for the leadership of the Ummah.

It is unacceptable for a Muslim who could, if he so wished, provide a cure for a patient at a public clinic or a charitable hospital to refuse to do so because he is waiting for an Islamic state to be established and provide such services. Nor would it be proper for a Muslim who could organize *zakah* services to be indifferent to the miseries and distresses of the poor, the orphaned, and the old and widowed, by simply hoping that the future Islamic state would help through a comprehensive system of social welfare. It is equally improper for a Muslim to show indifference to the tragic and costly disputes between other Muslims claiming that these matters will be dealt with by the future Islamic state, which will reconcile people and fight the aggressor.

On the contrary, the duty of the Muslim is to strive against evil and work for righteousness to the best of his abilities, no matter how little this might be. Allah (SWT) says in the Qur'ān: "So heed Allah as much as you can" (64:16).

The following may help to illustrate my concept regarding the desired Islamic state. An orchard of olive and palm trees takes a relatively long time to produce fruit. Is it then logical – or even practical – for the owner to do no other work, to reap no other fruit, but to only wait for a crop of the desired olives and dates? Of course not. He must plant other fast-producing trees as well as vegetables to fertilize his land and to earn a living, nurturing at the same time his olive and palm trees which will eventually provide his anticipated and desired crop.

5. My last paternal advice to young Muslims is to liberate themselves from the fetters of pessimism and despair and assume innocence and goodness in fellow Muslims. However, this optimism requires a conscious recognition of several important conditions:

First: Human beings are not angels. They have not been created from light, but molded from clay. They – like their father Ādam before them – are all fallible. We learn from the Qur'ān: "We had already, beforehand, taken the covenant of Ādam, but he forgot, and We found on his part no firm resolve" (20:115).

Recognition of our human fallibility and proclivity to temptation will enable us not only to tolerate and to cherish a sympathetic understanding of the faults and blemishes of others, but will move us to remind them to have faith and hope in Allah's mercy and to warn them of Allah's anger and of His punishment. Allah (SWT) addressed His Messenger, the Prophet Muḥammad (ṢAAS):

> Say: "O My Servants who have transgressed against their souls! Despair not of the mercy of Allah: for Allah forgives all sins: for He is Oft-forgiving, most Merciful" (39:53).

The possessive pronoun in "My servants" signifies Allah's love and concern for and indeed His benevolence toward human beings, which finds room for abundant mercy and forgivness for all sins however great they may be.

Second: It is imperative to understand that no one but Allah (SWT) knows what goes on in the innermost depths of a person. Therefore we are obliged to judge people in accordance with what they profess—what appears to us. If a person, for instance, confesses that "there is no god but Allah, and that Muḥammad is His Messenger," we should treat him as a Muslim. This is in keeping with the Prophet's *Sunnah*. He said:

> I have been ordered [by Allah (SWT)] to fight against the people until they testify that none has the right to be worshiped but Allah, and that Muḥammad is Allah's Messenger, and until they perform *ṣalawāt* perfectly and give *zakāh*. If they do all that, then they save their lives and property from me and they are accountable to Allah.

This is the reason why he would not punish the *munāfiqīn*, although he was sure they were plotting against him. When his companions suggested that he should kill them to preempt their threat, he replied: "I fear that the people would say that Muḥammad kills his companions!"

Third: We must recognize that every person who believes in Allah (SWT) and in His Messenger cannot be devoid of some inborn good, however evil his practice may be. Involvement in major transgressions does not uproot a person's *īmān* unless the transgressor deliberately defies Allah (SWT) and scorns His commands. Here, as elsewhere, we have to heed the *Sunnah* of the Prophet (ṢA'AS) who used to treat wrongdoers as a physician would treat a patient, not as a policeman would treat a criminal. He was very kind to them and always listened to their problems.

The following will, *in shā'a Allāh*, illustrate this point: A Qurayshī adolescent once came upon the Prophet (ṢA'AS) and asked permission to fornicate. The Prophet's companions were so outraged by the young man's request that they rushed to punish him, but the Prophet's attitude was totally different. Calm and composed he asked the young man to come closer to him and asked: "Would you approve of it [fornication] for your mother?" The young man replied: "No." The Prophet (ṢA'AS) said: "[Other] people also would not approve of it for their mothers." Then the Prophet (ṢA'AS) repeatedly asked the young man whether he would approve of it for his daughter, sister, or aunt? Each time the man answered "No," and each time the Prophet (ṢA'AS) added that "[Other] people would not approve of it for theirs." He then held the young man's hand and said: "May Allah forgive his [the young man's] sins, purify his heart, and fortify him [against such desires]."[22]

The Prophet's sympathetic attitude clearly indicates a gesture of goodwill, a conviction in that inborn goodness of man which outweighs the elements of evil which could only be transient. So he compassionately and patiently discussed the issue with him until he was able to convince him of its wrongfulness. Not only did he do that, but the Prophet (ṢA'AS) prayed to Allah to forgive and guide him. Extremists could argue that leniency on this occasion was understandable, as the young man had not actually committed fornication.

Let us, therefore, consider the following example: A married adulteress became pregnant, confessed her sin to the Prophet (ṢA'AS), and determinately and repeatedly insisted that she should be stoned to death to expiate her sin. When Khālid ibn al Walīd (RA'A) cursed her as she was being stoned, the Prophet (ṢA'AS) said to him: "Khālid, be gentle. By Him in whose hand is my life, she has made such repentance that even if a wrongful tax collector were to repent he would have been forgiven."[23]

Some may argue that this woman had transgressed but then repented. Here, therefore, is another example: During the lifetime of the Prophet (ṢA'AS) there was an alcoholic who was repeatedly brought to the Prophet (ṢA'AS) and was repeatedly punished, yet still persisted. One day when he was brought again on the same charge and was lashed, a man from among the people said: "May Allah curse him! How frequently has he been brought [to the Prophet (ṢA'AS) to be punished]?" The Prophet (ṢA'AS) said: "Do not curse him. By Allah I know he loves Allah and His Messenger." It is also reported that the Prophet (ṢA'AS) said: "Do not assist Satan against your brother."

The Prophet (ṢA'AS) prevented them from cursing him because their action could create discord and ill-feeling between the man and his Muslim brothers—his transgression should not sever the bond of brotherhood between him and other Muslims. Deep contemplation of the above examples and incidents amply demonstrates the Prophet's insight into the inherent element of goodness in man. We need, more than ever before, to study and follow the exemplary pattern that the Prophet (ṢA'AS) has set for us. Those extremists who indiscriminately accuse whoever makes a mistake of *kufr* or *shirk* must understand that they have to change their strategy and learn that a great deal of the corruption and

---

[22] Reported by Aḥmad and al Ṭabarānī as mentioned in *Majma' al Zāwā'id*, 1:129.

[23] Reported by Muslim and others.

perversion they abhor results mainly from ignorance of Islam, bad company, or forgetfulness. The solution is to to help people overcome and defeat all these problems. To be harsh, to accuse others of *kufr,* and to find fault with whatever they do only serves to alienate and estrange them. A wise man once said: "Rather than cursing darkness, try to light a candle for the road."

This is my advice for the enthusiastic and sincere young Muslims whom I hold very dear. My intention in all this is found in the following words of Prophet Shu'ayb ('AA) as revealed in the Qur'ān:

> I only desire [your] betterment to the best of my power; and my success [in my task] can only come from Allah. In Him I trust, and unto Him I look (11:88).

Index of Qur'anic Verses

5: Sūrat al Mā'idah

6: Sūrat al An'ām

7: Sūrat al A'rāf

8: Sūrat al Anfāl

Index of Hadith

General Index

Anas ibn Mālik, 25, 29, 30, 31, 122, 128, 140, 152
Anṣār, 42
Arabic language, 60, 122, 132
Arabs, 73, 80, 89, 114
arbitration, 67, 110
Aristotle, 87
Atatürk, 73, 93
atheism, 87
āyāt, 24

B

Badr, 143, 151, 161
Baghawī, al, 64
baghy, 109
Banū Qurayẓah, 118, 123
Bāqillānī, al, 111
basmalah, 125, 127
bāṭil, 12, 72, 73, 101, 103, 110, 143
Bayhaqī, al, 61, 121
beard, 30, 56, 105
Bedouin, 35
behavior, 21, 39, 49, 140
belief, 21, 37, 39, 60, 101, 140
bid'ah, 34, 50, 124, 126
blind, the, 162
Book, the, (see: Qur'an)
bribery, 84
Bukhārī, al, 58

C

Caesar, 86, 102
caliphate, 73, 78, 92, 123
caliphs, 151
Canada, 55
capitalism, 72
categorical texts, 66, 67
Catholic Church, 85
Catholic extremism, 106
charitable work, 163
Christian missionaries, 56

Freemason, 42

G
Genghiz Khān, 74
Ghazzālī, al, 111, 158
gold jewelry, 120, 121
good deeds, 26
Gourand, General, 90
Greek philosophy, 87
Graveyards, Muslim, 45
Gulf states, 31

H
hadith literature, 41, 43
Haḍramawt, 83
ḥajj, 22, 23, 52, 58, 63, 129
  types of, 126
ḥaqq, 143
Ḥajjāj ibn Yūsuf, al, 74, 86
ḥalāl, 30, 36, 57, 81, 93, 125, 130, 131
Ḥamzah, 126
ḥarām, 30, 57, 58, 78, 120, 125, 130, 131, 132
Hārūn, 40, 135
Ḥasan al Banna, 121, 122, 124, 153, 154
hady al tamattu', 52
Ḥāṭib, 160, 161
hereafter, 21, 23, 24
ḥayā', 61
ḥijāb, 30, 113
Hindu, 106
hippies, 107
historical materialism, 49
history, 74, 76, 77, 79
Hūlagū, 68
human nature, 39
humanity, 25
Ḥunayn, 143
Ḥusayn ibn 'Alī, al, 57, 74
hypocrisy, 60, 65

I

Israelites, 100
istiḥsān, 45

J
jāhilīyah, 60, 79, 125
Jamā'āt al Takfīr wa al Hijrah, 36, 77
jannah, 36, 77
Jawdat Sa'id, 140
Jews, 22, 57, 104, 106, 159
Jibrīl, 61, 62
jihad, 24, 41, 92, 93, 102, 103, 128, 138, 153, 163
jinn, 29
journalism, 116
judging by what Allah has revealed, 64, 65, 95
judgment, 103
justice, 21, 84, 100, 102, 103, 104

K
Ka'bah, 37, 53, 76, 125, 136, 143
Kabshah, 59
Karamīyah, 62
Khabāb ibn al Arat, 83
Khandaq, Battle of, 143
Khālid ibn al Walīd, 166
Khawārij, 43, 44, 68, 69, 70, 109, 110, 111
  Ḥarūrīyah, 69, 70
kindness, 39, 91
knowledge, 30, 50, 61, 68, 71, 72, 109, 112, 122, 128, 139, 152, 155
kufr, 30, 34, 41, 45, 60, 65, 68, 87, 93, 94, 95, 109, 111, 117, 128, 136, 143, 166
  definition of, 63

L
Labīd ibn Rabī'ah, 30
lamam, 132, 133
Lebanon, 88, 106
Legislation
  Allah's, 25
linguistics, 60
literalism, 51

literalists, 54, 154

M
Ma'mūn, al, 158
Madīnah, al, 133
maḥram, 52
Makkah, 53, 75, 76, 77, 160
makrūh, 60, 130
mandūb, 36
Marx, 92
Marxism, 83, 91
maṣlaḥah, 45
materialism, 24, 107
materialistic society, 37
meat
  eating of, 25
media, 84, 99
Messenger, the, 21, 27
middle course, 131
misinterpretation, 67, 69
missionaries, 56
moderation, 21
monasteries, 23
monasticism, 23
monotheism, 37, 81
moral conventions, 39
mosque, 37, 72, 74, 85, 101, 102, 110
mosquito, 57
mubāḥ, 60
Mu'ādh, 26, 35, 37, 156
Mu'āwiyah, 67
Mu'tazilah, 62
murder, 46, 117, 131
murtadd, 45 (see *riddah*)
Muṣ'ab, 152
Mūsā, 40, 135, 158
music, 32, 116
Muslim countries, 84, 90, 91, 101, 149
Muslim culture, 105
Muslim society, 41, 100

Muslim youth, 28, 103, 104, 105, 149, 159, 160, 161, 164, 167
Muslims, 21, 29, 30, 37, 57
Muṣṭafā, Shukrī, 77
mustaḥabb, 120
Muzdalifah, 22

N
Nasā'ī, al, 121
Nawawī, al, 22, 59
Nazism, 94
Negus, 138
New Testament, 86
nifāq, 60, 65, 66
non-Muslim, 157
non-Muslim countries, 36
North America, 37

O
oil revenues, 84
oppression, 94

P
paganism, 81, 136
Pakistan, 31, 72
Palestine, 88
parents, 159
People of the Book, 22, 57, 64, 138, 157
Persia, 114
personal freedom, 105
pessimism, 164
Pharaoh, 39, 40, 137, 158
Phillipines, 89, 106
photographs, 56
photography, 32, 116
pillars of Islam, 62, 110
politics, 50, 89, 102
polytheism, 76
pornographic material, 84
prison, 74, 93

produce, agricultural,
zakah on, 53, 54, 55
Prophet, the, 22, 23, 25, 26, 27, 28, 29, 33, 37, 38, 41, 45, 53, 54, 57, 66, 68, 76, 77, 82, 83, 84, 88, 91, 93, 99, 109, 114, 117, 118, 125, 126, 128, 136, 144, 149, 151, 153, 156, 157, 159, 165, 166
wives of, 19, 105

Q
Qatādah, 64
qiṣāṣ, 155
qiyām, 44
qiyās, 45, 51, 119
qunūt, 126
Qur'an, the, 27, 52, 132
Qur'anic sciences, 112
Qur'anic trandation, 52
Quraysh, 80, 160

R
Rāfiḍī, 28
Ramaḍan, 52, 63, 124, 129
Rashīd, Harūn al, 127
rationalism, 137
reconciliation between husband and wife, 68
regime, 154
rijāl al Dīn, 150
religion, 21, 22, 24, 49
religious extremism, (see extremism)
religious practice, 23, 37
religious society, 29
respect for elders, 160
revelation, 69
revolt, 95
rhetoric, 154
riddah, 63, 87, 95, 136
rijāl al dīn, 150

S
Sa'd al Dīn Ibrāhīm, 104
Sa'īd ibn Jubayr, 74

Sa'īd ibn al Musayyib, 152
ṣadaqah, 161, 162
ṣalah, 23, 26, 35, 36, 42, 52, 62, 69, 76, 81, 105, 110, 116, 118, 123, 126, 128, 129, 130, 139, 143, 151, 156, 162, 165
ṣalāt al 'aṣr, 118
ṣalāt al fajr, 35, 125
ṣalāt al jumu'ah, 36, 52, 130
ṣalāt al tarāwīḥ, 124
Salmān al Fārisī, 27
Ṣan'ā', 83
Satan, 22, 42, 72, 114, 153, 166
Saudi Arabia, 31
schism, 50
secular philosophies, 84
secular sciences, 153
secularism, 56, 83, 86, 87, 135
Shāfi'ī, al, 28, 31, 122, 127, 128
Shari'ah, 28, 31, 33, 38, 44, 46, 51, 53, 55, 57, 62, 64, 67, 71, 72,74, 76, 84, 85, 92, 93, 94, 101, 102, 103, 112, 113, 116, 117, 118, 124, 125, 128, 135, 137, 138, 145, 149, 150, 163, 180
Shāṭibī, al, 50, 68, 69, 112
Shawkānī, al, 110
Shaykh Shukrī, (see Muṣṭafā Shukrī)
shirk, 43, 70, 136, 166
  major and minor, 65
Shu'ayb, 39, 167
ṣirāṭ al mustaqīm, al, 21
siwāk, 105
ṣiyām, 23, 27, 28, 29, 36, 43, 52, 63, 81, 104, 129, 138, 155, 157
social injustices, 84
social issues, 103
social welfare, 149, 164
socialism, 71
society, 39, 49, 76, 100, 149
Somalia, 88
sorcery, 131
spirituality, 24
spoils of war, 42
Sufis, 130
Sufism, 154

Sufyān al Thawrī, 155
sunan, 49, 76, 78, 81, 82, 118, 139, 142, 143
Sunnah, 25, 27, 29, 31, 33, 34, 36, 41, 46, 54, 58, 68, 72, 76, 86, 92, 100, 112, 113, 115, 117, 119, 123, 124, 127, 129, 130, 150, 153, 154, 155, 158, 160, 165
suspicion among extremists, 42
sword, 45
Syria, 115

T

takfīr, 14, 67, 94
ṭawāf, 76
tawḥīd, al, 64
Ṭāwūs, 64
ta'līl al aḥkām, 51
ṭayyibāt, al, 23, 24, 28
texts, 66, 67, 113, 117, 123, 154, 159
Thamūd, 39
Thawbān, 120
Tirmidhī, al, 54, 59
Torah, 100
torture, 93, 94, 107
tradition, 31, 103
translation, Qur'ānic, (see Qur'ānic translation)
trust, 51
truth, 22, 36, 39
Turkey, 73, 92
tyranny, 158
tyrants, 75

U

Uḥud, 75, 78
'ulama, 31, 32, 44, 51, 70, 71, 72, 73, 109, 110, 124, 125, 139, 151, 153
'Umar ibn 'Abd al 'Azīz, 55, 81, 118, 138
'Umar ibn al Khaṭṭāb, 26, 33, 59, 69, 102, 107, 108, 124, 125, 133, 134, 151, 160
Ummah, 11, 21, 28, 32, 42, 43, 50, 56, 74, 83, 85, 88, 90, 91, 101, 116, 118, 119, 122, 128, 132, 133, 139, 145, 163
  consensus of, 33
United Nations, 90

IIIT ENGLISH PUBLICATIONS

A. Islamization of Knowledge Series

- *The Islamic Theory of International Relations: New Directions for Islamic Methodology and Thought* (1407/1987) by Dr. 'AbdulḤamīd AbūSulaymān.
- *Islamization of Knowledge: General Principles and Work Plan*, 3rd edition (1409/1989).
- *Toward Islamic Anthropology: Definitions, Dogma, and Directions* (1406/1986) by Dr. Akbar S. Aḥmad.
- *Toward Islamic English* (1406/1986) by Dr. Ismā'īl Rājī al Fārūqī.
- *Modeling-Interest Free Economy: A Study in Microeconomics and Development* (1407/1987) by Dr. Muḥammad Anwar.
- *Islam: Source and Purpose of Knowledge*. Papers presented at the Second International Conference of Islamic Thought and the Islamization of Knowledge (1409/1988).
- *Toward Islamization of Disciplines*. Papers presented in 1402/1982 at the Third International Conference on Islamic Thought and the Islamization of Knowledge (1409/1988).
- *The Organization of the Islamic Conference: An Introduction to an Islamic Political Institution* (1408/1988) by Dr. 'Abdullāh al Aḥsan.
- *Proceedings of the Lunar Calendar Conference*. Papers presented at the Conference of the Lunar Calendar. Edited by Dr. Imād ad-Deen Aḥmad (1408/1988).
- *Islamization of Attitudes and Practices in Science and Technology,* papers presented at a conference on the same topic (1409/1989). Edited by Dr. M.A.K. Lodhi.

B. Issues in Contemporary Islamic Thought Series

- *Islamic Thought and Culture*, papers presented to the Islamic Studies Group of the American Academy of Religion (1402/1982). Edited by Dr. Ismā'īl Rājī al Fārūqī.

- *Trialogue of the Abrahamic Faiths*, 2nd edition (1406/1986). Papers presented to the Islamic Studies Group of the American Academy of Religion. Edited by Dr. Ismā'īl Rājī al Fārūqī.

- *Islamic Awakening: Between Rejection and Extremism* by Dr. Yūsuf al Qaraḍāwī. Published jointly with the American Trust Publications. (new revised edition, 1412/1992)

- *Tawḥīd: Its Implications for Thought and Life* by Dr. Ismā'īl Rājī al Fārūqī (second edition, 1412/1992).

C. Research Monographs Series

- *Uṣūl al Fiqh al Islāmī: Source Methodology in Islamic Jurisprudence* (1411/1990) by Dr. Ṭāhā Jābir al 'Alwānī.

- *Islam and the Middle East: The Aesthetics of a Political Inquiry* (1411/1990) by Dr. Mona Abul-Fadl.

- *Sources of Scientific Knowledge: The Concept of Mountains in the Qur'an* (1411/1991) Dr. Zaghloul R. El-Naggar.

D. Occasional Papers Series

- *Outlines of A Cultural Strategy* (1410/1989) by Dr. Ṭāhā Jābir al 'Alwānī. [A French edition was published under the title *Pour une Strategie Culturelle Islamique* (1411/1990)].

- *Islamization of Knowledge: A Methodology* (1412/1991) by Dr. 'Imād al Dīn Khalil [A French edition was published under the title (*Methodologic Pour Islamization du Savior* (1412-1991)].

- *The Qur'an and the Sunnah: The Time Space Factor* (1412/1991) by Dr. Ṭāhā Jābir al 'Alwānī and Dr. 'Imād al Dīn Khalīl.

E. Human Development Series

- *Training Guide for Islamic Workers* by Dr. Hisham Altalib, second revised edition, 1412-1992.

F. Perspectives on Islamic Thought Series:

- *National Security and Development Strategy* (1412-1991) by Arshad Zaman.

Distributors of IIIT Publications

To order IIIT Publications write to:

North America
Islamic Book Service
10900 W. Washington St.
Indianapolis, IN 46231 U.S.A.
Tel: (317) 839-9248
Fax: (317) 839-2511

Al Sa'dāwi / United Arab Bureau
P.O. Box 4059
Alexandria, VA 22303 USA
Tel: (703) 329-6333
Fax: (703) 329-8052

Egypt
IIIT Office
26-B Al Jazirah al Wusṭa St.
Zamalek, Cairo
Tel: (202) 340-9520
Fax: (202) 340-9520

Jordan
IIIT Office
P.O. Box 9489, Amman
Tel: (962-6) 639-992
Fax: (962-6) 611-420

Lebanon
United Arab Bureau
P.O. Box 135788
Beirut
Tel: 807-779
Telex: 21665 LE

Europe and United Kingdom
Muslim Information Centre
233 Seven Sisters Rd.
London N4 2DA
Tel: (44-71) 272-5170
Fax: (44-71) 272-3214

The Islamic Foundation
Markfield Da'wah Centre, Rutby Lane
Markfield, Leicester LE6 ORN, U.K.
Tel: (44-530) 244-944/45
Fax: (44-530) 244-946

India
Genuine Publications & Media (Pvt.) Ltd.
P.O. Box 9725
Jamia Nagar
New Delhi 110 025
Tel: (91-11) 630-989
Fax: (91-11) 684-1104

Saudi Arabia
International House for Islamic Books
P.O. Box 55195, Riyadh 11534
Tel: (966) 1-465-0818
Fax: (966) 1-463-3489

Morocco
Dar al Aman for Publishing and Distribution
4 Zangat al Ma'muniyah
Rabat
Tel: (212) 7-723-276